Marked States

Volume 3

The Harvard Psilocybin Project
1960-1963

Marked States Series Editor   Randolph Dible
                                                    randolphdible@gmail.com

The Harvard Psilocybin Project 1960-1963

Edward J. Reither

"It is fitting and natural that the Harvard intellectual community be the first to grapple with this new philosophic and practical issue and that the University of William James be given the first chance to accept or reject the educational potentialities of consciousness-expanding drugs."

Richard Alpert and Timothy Leary,
December 13, 1962, Harvard Crimson

ISBN 978-1-84890-489-7

College Publications
Scientific Director: Dov Gabbay
Managing Director: Jane Spurr

http://www.collegepublications.co.uk

Cover produced by Laraine Welch

Dedicated to my muse

Liisa

Table of Contents

"Ego or the sense of "I" in terms of the structures, patterns, abstractions by which one defines himself. It seemed to me that these were being dissociated in me, and I as a knower was unable to confirm my knowing or to sustain my sense of identity by referring to any stable elements of myself. I recall looking at a Buddhist symbol, a circle divided into two S-shaped parts, one black and one white, with a center in each of the semicircles which formed the 'S'. I struggled to bring the two centers together, as if "the I" had to do so to survive. I can remember twisting and straining with all my might, saying "I-I-I-I-I" and somehow being aware that the matter of my universe was to maintain the "I" while all else was stripped away."

Harvard Psilocybin Project participants report, 1961

Introduction

Embark on a fascinating journey into the annals of history with our course, "The Harvard Psilocybin Project, 1960 to 1963," a captivating exploration that was offered by the Harvard Institute for Learning and Retirement during the fall of 2023. Delve into the profound and tumultuous story of a groundbreaking initiative initiated by Timothy Leary, Frank Barron, and Richard Alpert, known as Ram Dass, as they sought to unravel the therapeutic potential of psychedelic drugs. This course unfolds the remarkable narrative of the Harvard Psilocybin Project, a pivotal chapter in American history that sparked a cultural revolution and now, more than 60 years later, resurfaces as a respected realm of research and therapeutic promise.

At the core of this venture was the revelation that psilocybin, the mind-expanding mushroom, exposed hidden realms to ordinary waking consciousness. The project, once a beacon of exploration, administered nearly 400 trials to willing and informed participants, including creative artists, poets, authors, and university professors. However, the project's trajectory took an unexpected turn, challenging the stability and authority of Harvard University under the direction of Harvard's Center for Personality Research. Following three tumultuous years, the project was shut down, leading to the dismissal of Harvard professors Timothy Leary and Richard Alpert, both cast under the spotlight of national media coverage.

Why does this course hold such significance today? The legacy of the Harvard Psilocybin Project extends far beyond its origins, influencing contemporary research and therapeutic applications of psychedelic substances. Harvard Medical School, Massachusetts General Hospital, and Harvard Law School have embraced this field, actively pursuing research, legal considerations, and health policy advancements related to psilocybin. The Harvard Divinity School, in collaboration with the Center for the Study of World Religion, engages with the Harvard Psychedelic Project,

1

shedding light on the intricate intersections of psychedelics, religion, and spirituality.

As we unravel the layers of the Harvard Psilocybin Project, we discover it as a product of its time—an outgrowth of scientific, religious, psychological, philosophical, and cultural evolution that transcended deeply entrenched 19th and 20th-century beliefs. This course, which you are about to embark upon, will meticulously explore the three transformative years within the Harvard Center for Personality Research, examining the ripple effects across various university departments and the broader academic, social, and political landscape.

Uncover the rich history of mind-expanding substances, tracing their evolution from societal shadows to the forefront of academic, scientific, legal, psychological, and medical discussions.

The discovery of mind-expanding substances such as psilocybin, mescaline, and LSD in the 1960s was a significant event in the history of human thinking. It challenged the established order of post-World War II culture and threatened the traditional beliefs and understanding of how the world was supposed to operate. The documentation of experimentation with these substances can be traced back to Germany after the war when scientists tested them on prisoners to control their minds. However, the use of these substances by musicians, poets, authors, and intellectuals in North America and Europe brought about a new understanding of the human mind and consciousness. Even though the Harvard Psilocybin Project was shut down, discovering and exploring these substances continued, opening up new avenues of human thinking and understanding.

That God Dammed School

"That God damned School / They're trying to change me. / They just want to kill my character" - "Well, don't let them"!!

Timothy Leary's letter to David Mc Clelland

LUNDSGADE 4
COPENHAGEN

Oct 3, 1959

Dear M's,

The optimistic tone of your last letter was heartening, indicating to me that the effects of our favorite brand of geographical therapy tend to be durable. I am counting on you to keep it up. To paraphrase that great beatnik bard, KM, "that God damned School/ They're trying to change me./ They just want to kill my character...."

Well, don't let them !!!

Actually Copehhagen is giving us a taste of USA. As you know Gerhart is a great politician and he has lined up a busy speaking schedule for me including a seminar with the top graduate students to whom I am presenting my book. Its a valuable preview,in the nature of a Bridgeport opening and I rush home after each meeting to revise Chapters. I see "my flesh disappear down the aluminum throat, and I didn't care". I just revise.

4

The Harvard Psilocybin Project
1960-63

"When Hiroshima was destroyed by an atomic bomb in 1945, it is said, the first living thing to emerge from the blasted landscape was a ...mushroom."

Anna Lowenhaupt Tsing, The Mushroom at the End of the World (Princeton: Princeton Press, 2015).

Timothy Leary, Frank Barron, and Richard Alpert (Ram Dass) founded the Harvard Psilocybin Project in 1960 to research the therapeutic effects of psychedelic drugs. They discovered the drug's effect depended primarily on the 'set' of the person's present state of mind and the setting or environment. Psilocybin opens up what is usually 'hidden' to ordinary waking consciousness, which can be enlightening but also terrifying.

The project is said to have administered (documented) close to 400 trials to willing and informed students, participants, creative artists, poets, authors, and university professors. Unfortunately, the project, under the guidance and direction of Harvard's Center for Personality Research, became problematic and threatened the stability and authority of the university.

After three tremulous years the project was shut down, and two Harvard professors were dismissed under widespread national news.

Harvard Crimson

CAMBRIDGE, MASS., TUESDAY, MAY 28, 1963   TEN CENTS

Corporation Fires Richard Alpert For Giving Undergraduates Drugs

First Dismissal Under Pusey

By JOSEPH M. RUSSIN and ANDREW T. WEIL

The Corporation has terminated the appointment of Richard Alpert as assistant professor of Clinical Psychology and of Education for violating a University agreement by giving consciousness-expanding drugs to an undergraduate, President Pusey told the CRIMSON yesterday.

Pusey also said that Timothy F. Leary, Lecturer on Clinical Psychology, was relieved of his teaching duties and had his salary terminated on April 30 for leaving Cambridge and his classes without permission.

In his statement to the CRIMSON, Pusey said Alpert had violated an agreement with the University not to give consciousness-expanding drugs such as psilocybin and mescaline to undergraduates. The statement also implied that Alpert had lied to an officer of the University last November when he "assured" the Administration that "he had not given drugs to any undergraduate."

Alpert's appointment as assistant professor of Clinical Psychology was to have expired June 30, but he also held an appointment through next year at the School of Education. The Corporation's action terminated both of these appointments effective immediately.

The Harvard Psilocybin Project was not only about Harvard, a mind-expanding mushroom, or a single study conducted at one of the country's most elite and prestigious universities. The project represented a moment in American history that exploded into a cultural revolution that is only now beginning to return after more than 60 years as a respectable and valuable areas of research.

Today, Harvard Medical School and Massachusetts General Hospital have an active Psilocybin research center and clinic administering psilocybin as an effective medication for many serious emotional and physical disorders. The Harvard Law School has a program devoted to Psychedelic Law and Regulation at the Petrie-Flom Center for Health Law Policy. Harvard Divinity School and its Center for the Study of World Religion regularly work with The Harvard Psychedelic Project. This student organization

6

holds nationwide conferences at the university on how psychedelics, religion, and spirituality work together.

When we look at The Harvard Psilocybin Project of 1960 today, we can see it was an outgrowth and an emergence of a scientific, religious, psychological, philosophical, and cultural evolution (r-evolution) that was exploding and transcending 19th and 20th century deeply held institutional and religious beliefs. This program will explore and develop these and other significant areas of yesterday's and today's understanding.

This course will focus on the three years it ran at Harvard's Center for Personality Research and other departments within the University, along with other academic, social, and political controversies it created. In addition, the course will consider the history of mind-expanding substances and recent research in academic, scientific, legal, psychological, and medical fields - while discussing current thinking about psilocybin and mind-expanding substances in general. Our sessions will include lectures, video presentations, discussions of the readings, and a guest speaker, Gunther Weil, the last remaining member of the project.

The Setting

An Era of Promise

Harvard students – 1960

9

Current Conversations

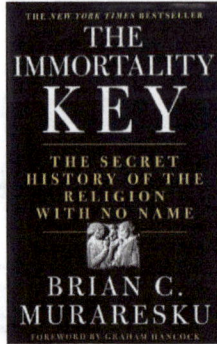

Mark J. Plotkin talks with Brian C. Muraresku

Mark J. Plotkin, a Harvard and Yale-trained ethnobotanist, and Brian C. Murakesk, author of 'The Immortality Key'

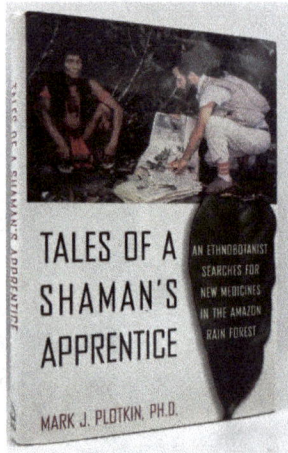

"I don't know why it's taken 60 years."

Mark J. Plotkins: So I want to wind up here with a bit of a loaded question, which goes back to something we touched on, and that is the history of hallucinogens in Harvard, which is something which has been fascinating me for 40 years. Many people think that hallucinogens and their study began with Leary and Alpert, God forbid, in the '60s. More of us in the know like to think it began with Schultes in the '30s and '40s. Those of us who've really dug deeper, like you and I, know it began with William James prior to the turn of the century. But I'd like to know your perspective, having spent so much time at my old alma mater, as the contributions and the mistakes made by Leary and Alpert, which very few people address these days, where people continue to lionize them without calling attention to the pitfalls that they did fall into.

Brian Muraresku: That is a loaded question. Yeah, I haven't talked about this publicly, but Leary is still a bit of a four letter word on campus, and just in generality has been having, I mentioned these conversations with folks from the divinity school to the law school to the medical school to the faculty of arts and sciences, just that there's a lot of genuine organic interest in this topic. And I noticed over the past couple years that the specter of Leary, the shadow of Leary kind of hangs in the corner of every conversation. Because for those who don't know, the pied piper of psychedelic enlightenment, Mr. Leary, gets a lot of flack for what happened at Harvard in the early 1960s.

And when he and Dick Alpert, who became Ram Dass were kicked off campus, that was the beginning of a long hiatus in these studies. So we're talking about, this is about 60 years. So from 1962 until where we sit today, it's been a full 60 years since some of this controversy erupted. But like we talked about at the very beginning, despite that psychic load, I think that the clinical work certainly made an impact.

Source: Tim Ferriss Show, December 29, 2022

11

Background

Wade Davis, Ethnobotanist and author of 'The Wayfinders', 'The Serpent and the Rainbow', talking with Mark Hyman, M.D. of the Ultra Wellness Center and author of 'The Doctors Farmacy'

(17:50)

Introduction

Video link

https://youtu.be/ZGtdeTUJCzg

Wade Davis, Ethnobotanist and author of 'The Wayfinders', 'The Serpent and the Rainbow', talking with Mark Hyman, M.D. of the Ultra Wellness Center and author of 'The Doctors Farmacy' - What Ancient Cultures Have to Teach PUs about Plant Medicine & Psychedelics - June 29, 2022

A Look Back

Under what authority did early Spanish explorers sail under?

Marina (mistress and mother) and Hernán Cortés

14

Papal Bulls

Papal Bulls

Obverse side of the seal of Pope Martin V. Notice the dots in the hair and beard of Saint Peter on the left. University Archives KU Leuven, Archives of the Old University of Leuven

(letters of decree/charter)

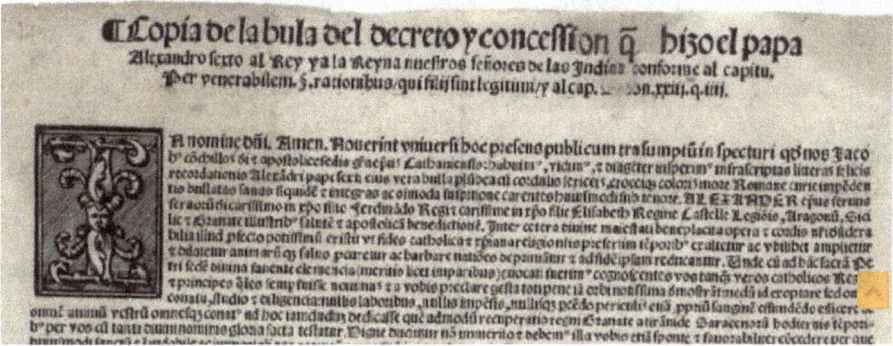

Edits that created the foundation of the Doctrine of *Discovery*

Requerimiento - 1510

Document written by jurist Palacios Rubios, of the Council of Castille.

On the part of the King, Don Fernando, and of Doña Juana, his daughter, Queen of Castille and León, subduers of the barbarous nations, we their servants notify and make known to you, as best we can, that the Lord our God, Living and Eternal, created the Heaven and the Earth, and one man and one woman, of whom you and we, all the men of the world, were and are descendants, and all those who came after us. But, on account of the multitude which has sprung from this man and woman in the five thousand years since the world was created, it was necessary that some men should go one way and some another, and that they should be divided into many kingdoms and provinces, for in one alone they could not be sustained.

Of all these nations God our Lord gave charge to one man, called St. Peter, that he should be Lord and Superior of all the men in the world, that all should obey him, and that he should be the head of the whole human race, wherever men should live, and under whatever law, sect, or belief they should be; and he gave him the world for his kingdom and jurisdiction.

And he commanded him to place his seat in Rome, as the spot most fitting to rule the world from; but also he permitted him to have his seat in any other part of the world, and to judge and govern all Christians, Moors, Jews, Gentiles, and all other sects. This man was called Pope, as if to say, Admirable Great Father and Governor of men. The men who lived in that time obeyed that St. Peter, and took him for Lord, King, and Superior of the universe; so also they have regarded the others who after him have been elected to the pontificate, and so has it been continued even till now, and will continue till the end of the world.

16

Key Points

1. **Cultural Sensitivity and Respect**: One moral lesson is the importance of cultural sensitivity and respect when encountering new cultures and traditions. Spanish explorers arrived in the Americas with the aim of spreading Christianity, but they encountered indigenous peoples with their own belief systems and practices. Rather than immediately demonizing these practices, there could have been an effort to understand and respect the indigenous cultures.

2. **Religious Tolerance**: This story highlights the tension between religious beliefs and religious tolerance. The Christian monks' decision to label the sacred mushrooms as the work of the devil and eliminate their use raises questions about religious intolerance and the imposition of one's beliefs on others. A more tolerant approach might have involved dialogue and discussion rather than suppression.

3. **Ethical Use of Resources**: The discovery of sacred mushrooms also raises ethical questions about the use of natural resources. It's important to consider whether the exploitation or destruction of valuable resources, whether they are cultural or environmental, is ethically justifiable.

4. **Unintended Consequences**: This story reminds us of the unintended consequences of actions taken with good intentions. The suppression of indigenous practices could have led to a loss of cultural heritage and could have had negative impacts on indigenous communities.

5. **Historical Perspective**: Lastly, this story underscores the importance of studying history to learn from past mistakes and actions. Understanding the complexities of historical events can help us make more informed decisions in the present and avoid repeating similar mistakes.........

The Mushrooms Origin

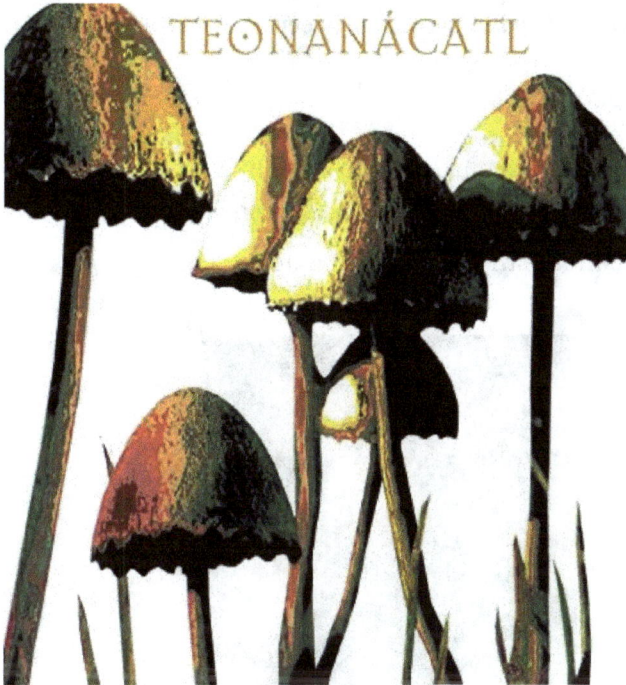

TEONANÁCATL

Teonanacatl

The term *Teonanácatl* (te-on-a-na-catl), an Aztec word translated as "sacred mushroom" or "God's flesh," was first documented by Spanish chroniclers in the sixteenth century. Alongside peyotl and ololiuqui, *Teonanácatl* became a subject of fascination for the Spanish, who were trying to understand the native customs of the New World. One of the most important sources of information on these sacred mushrooms comes from Bernardino de Sahagún's renowned chronicle *Historia General de las Cosas de Nueva España*, written between 1529 and 1590.

1560

Spanish priest Bernardino de Sahagún wrote in his *Florentine Codex* about the use of peyote and teonanacatl mushrooms by the Aztecs.

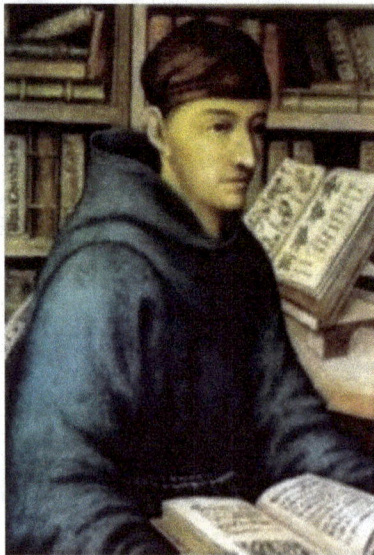

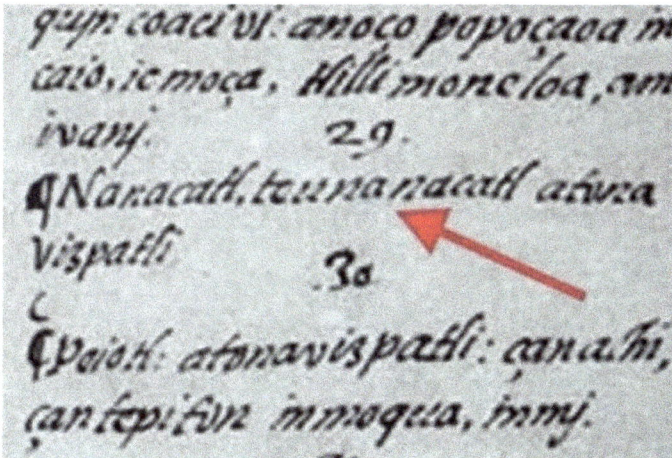

This work remains a key historical document for understanding indigenous practices, including the use of entheogenic substances like mushrooms.

Sahagún was not alone in recording observations about the use of these mushrooms in Mesoamerica. Other significant figures who wrote about *Teonanácatl* included Francisco Hernández, a physician to the King of Spain, and friars Diego Durán and Bernardino Sahagún, both of whom came from families of converted Jews. These scholars noted the ritualistic importance of these mushrooms among the indigenous peoples, though often their accounts were brief and lacking in detail.

By the eighteenth century, references to these mushrooms had all but disappeared. After 1727, documentation of *Teonanácatl* became sparse, with only a single trivial mention over the next two centuries. Remarkably, even one prominent Mesoamerican scholar seemed to forget that these sacred mushrooms had ever existed, indicating how thoroughly knowledge of these entheogens had been erased from the historical record for a significant period.

Origin and meaning of the term Teonanacatl

https://canvas.harvard.edu/courses/120100/pages/teonanacatl

Teonanácatl, a sixteenth century Indian drawing from
the Magliabechiano Codex. Redrawn by E. W. Smith

Florentine Codex, Book 11, by Bernadino de Sahagun

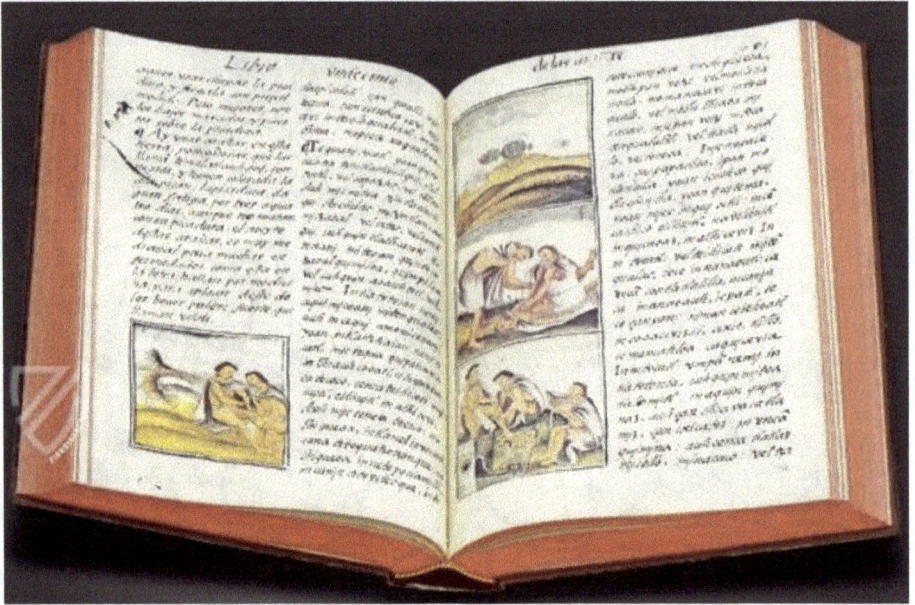

The book contains data on the use of intoxicating sacred mushrooms which were eaten by the Indians of Mexico at their feasts and religious ceremonies. From the Sahagun's chronicle and from other reports it can be seen that teonanácatl was not only ingested at social and festival occasions but also by witch doctors and soothsayers. The mushroom god-which the Christian missionaries called the devil, endowed them with clairvoyant properties, which enabled them, besides other things, to identify the causes of diseases and indicate the way in which they could be treated.

The Age of the Mushrooms

Martin Terry, Karen   L. Steelman, Tom Guilderson, Phil Dering, Marvin W. Rowe

Journal of Archaeological Science
Volume 33, Issue 7, July 2006, Pages 1017-1021

ELSEVIER

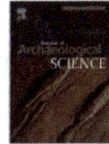

Abstract

This study demonstrates the use of peyote by inhabitants of the Lower Pecos region of the Chihuahuan Desert about 6000 calendar years ago, and confirms its use by inhabitants of the Cuatro Ciénegas region of the Chihuahuan Desert in Late Prehistoric times. The Shumla Caves' specimens are composed of an aggregate of ground peyote mixed with other plant material, i.e., they appear to be manufactured peyote effigies, and are definitely not intact peyote buttons.

Peyote, a psychoactive cactus native to the Chihuahuan Desert *(6000 years ago)*, has been preserved from excavations at only two archaeological sites: Shumla Caves in the Lower Pecos region of southwest Texas and shelter CM-79 near Cuatro Ciénegas in Coahuila, Mexico.

We determined three indistinguishable radiocarbon ages of 5160 ± 45, 5200 ± 35, and 5210 ± 35 ^{14}C years BP, yielding a mean age of 5195 ± 20 ^{14}C years BP for the three specimens from Shumla Caves. For one of the Cuatro Ciénegas specimens, we obtained the first direct radiocarbon date of 835 ± 35 ^{14}C years BP.

25

Few plants of the gods have ever been held in greater reverence than the sacred mushrooms of Mexico. So hallowed were these fungi that the Aztecs called them Teonanacatl ("divine flesh") and used them only in the most holy of their ceremonies. Even though, as fungi, mushrooms do not blossom, the Aztecs referred to them as "flower," and the Indians who still use them in religious rituals have endearing terms for them, such as "little flowers."

Above: One of the largest fruiting bodies of *Psilocybe azurescens* ever found.

When the Spaniards conquered Mexico, they were horrified to discover that the indigenous people used intoxicating plants, such as peyotl, ololiuqui, and teonanácatl, in their religious rituals.

The use of mushrooms in particular was deeply offensive to the European ecclesiastical authorities, who immediately set out to eliminate them from indigenous spiritual practices.

One chronicler wrote, "They had another method of intoxication, which heightened their cruelty. By consuming small toadstools, they would experience visions—often of snakes. They called these mushrooms *teonanácatl* in their language, meaning 'God's flesh,' or possibly of the Devil, whom they worshiped. In this way, with this bitter food, they partook in communion with their cruel god."

In 1656, a guide for missionaries argued against Indian idolatries, including mushroom ingestion, and recommended their extirpation. Not only do reports condemn Teonanacatl, but actual illustrations also denounce it. One depicts the devil enticing an Indian to eat the fungus; another has the devil performing a dance upon a mushroom.

Dr. Francisco Hernandez, personal physician to the king of Spain, wrote that three kinds of intoxicating mushrooms were worshiped. After describing a lethal species, he stated that "others when eaten cause not death but madness that on occasion is lasting, of which the symptom is a kind of uncontrolled laughter.

For four centuries nothing was known of the mushroom cult; and it was even doubted that mushrooms were used hallucinogenically in ceremony. The Church fathers had done such a successful job of driving the cult into hiding through persecution that no anthropologist or botanist had ever uncovered the religious use of these mushrooms until this century.

Plants of the Gods, Their Sacred, Healing, and Hallucinogenic Powers, p. 158.

28

Louis Lewin - *(pronounced Leveen)*

Father of Toxicology

There is probably no more serviceable classification of the plant's man uses in his striving for temporary relief from reality than that proposed by the German Toxicologist, Louis Lewin.

Of Lewin's five categories, i.e., Excitantia, Inebriantia, Hypontical, Euporica, Phantastica, none has stirred deeper interest through the ages, and none has foretokened a greater field for discovery for the present and future, that the Phantastica. There have recently been proposed very learned and intricate words to distinguish the several kinds of narcotics.

29

Our modern terminology has come to call these the hallucinogens, the psychotomimeties, or the psychedelics.

He spent a lifetime studying morphine and cocaine, mescaline from Anhalonium Lewinii (the peyote plant, named after him by Hennings), the harmala alkaloids, Piper methysticum (kava kava), and Chavica betel. And he left a legacy of almost 300 journal publications and several monographs on toxicological, forensic, ethnographic, pharmacological, and historical topics.

Taken from lectures given by Richard Evans Schultes, Ph.D. Curator of Economic Botany, Botanical Museum of Harvard University in the Third Lecture Series 1960, College of Pharmacy, University of Texas.

The Age of Promise

We see the past as the future will see us.
the *Lantingxu* 兰亭序

The above quotation comes from the *Foreword to the Orchid Pavilion* (*Lantingxu*), written by Wang Xizhi 王羲之 (321–379), the most celebrated calligrapher in Chinese history. It subtly warns against making hasty judgement before one understands the historical, social and cultural background of the subject in question.

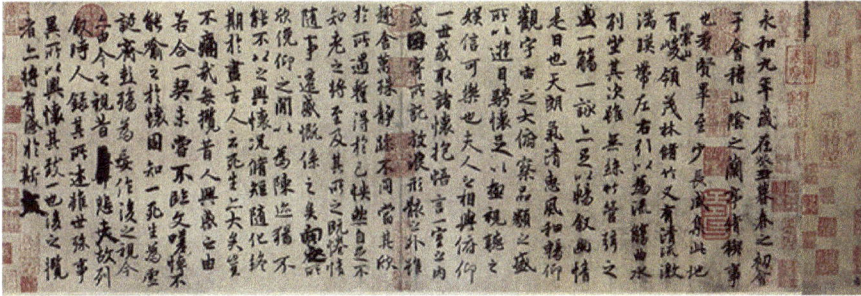

A Tang Dynasty copy of the *Preface to the Poems Composed at the Orchid Pavilion*, written in fourth century by the "Sage of Calligraphy," Wang Xizhi.

The relationship Harvard holds with psychedelics is long, convoluted, and until recently, static in its progression. Many are familiar with psychedelics' fall to social damnation during the '60s, less are familiar with how institutions like Harvard were involved, and less still are familiar with academia's attitude towards these compounds before the research ceased.

When the history of psychedelics at Harvard is recited, it is often oversaturated with retellings of Timothy Leary and Richard Alpert's infamous Psilocybin Project. During its time, the Harvard Psilocybin Project was likely the most high-profile, public-facing psychedelic research project that had ever been undertaken. But just two years later, the project was terminated – permanently tainting not just the public, but also academia's perception of the substances. However, in the years before controversy halted psychedelic research, it was a different story.

Harvard Independent, Christian Browder, March 11, 202

"I predict that within one generation we will have across the bay in Berkeley a Department of Psychedelic Studies."

Timothy Leary, The Politics of Ecstasy, 1965

The Project

1960

Harvard Students 1961

Harvard *is where everyone in any academic or professional activity in the Boston area has one way of measuring his success. Can he get on the Harvard payroll? The word Harvard in the Boston area is a powerful status symbol operating at every societal level. There are several thousand janitors around the Boston area, but if you are a janitor at Harvard, you're a prince among custodians. The same with a cook, the same with a gardener, the same with a psychologist.*

Timothy Leary, *High Priest*

33

Harvard College during the 1950s appeared in many ways to return to its prewar state. Only about a quarter of the students in 1958 were on financial aid. The typical graduate five years out in the mid-fifties lived in a large northeastern city, was married with one child, was a Republican who went to church once a month. Most undergraduates sought to live up to their national billing as the elite of the elite. The dress-down clothing style of the postwar vets gave way to resurgent preppy attire: casually (that is, purposefully) dirtied white buckskin shoes, tweed jackets, green book bags, and alpine parkas. "At a distance and even from quite close up," said one observer, "everyone looks alike." The prevailing social style was "polite arrogance—spare, dry, cautious, and angular."

Making Harvard Modern: The Rise of America's University

Morton Keller and Phyllis Keller

Harvard Players

Robert Gordon Wasson (Botany fellow)

Richard Evens Schultes (Botany Professor)

Timothy Leary (Harvard lecturer)

Frank Barron (visiting Professor - Berkeley)

David McClelland – (Harvard Professor) - Department of Social Relations director)

Richard Alpert (Ram Dass) (Harvard Professor)

Ralph Metzner (Graduate Student)

Gunther Weil (Graduate Student)

Henry Murray (Harvard Professor)

Herb Kelman (Harvard Professor)

Christina Morgan (Research assistant)

Andrew Weil (Graduate student)

Aldous Huxley (Author)

Huston Smith (M.I.T. Professor)

and more

The Beats

Brief Timeline

The Harvard Psilocybin Project 1960-1962

Spring 1959

Meets McClelland in Florence, Italy by Frank Barron and is offered a position as a lecturer at Harvard in Existential Transactional Analysis and Methods

Fall 1959

Starts teaching at Harvard

Meets Richard Alpert

Invites Frank Barron to come to Harvard

Summer 1960

Timothy Leary takes visionary mushrooms, known to the Aztecs as Teonanacatl, in Cuernavaca, Mexico. He returns to Harvard University and together with fellow faculty members Frank Barron and Richard Alpert and several graduate students, initiates research projects with psilocybin, the psychoactive ingredient of the mushroom, supplied by Sandoz Pharmaceuticals.

Fall 1960

Aldous Huxley, then visiting lecturer at MIT, and Huston Smith, professor of religion at MIT, became involved with the project as consultants and advisors. Poets Allen Ginsberg and Peter Orlovsky visit, take psilocybin and become allies and supporters of the project. They take Leary to turn on Beatnik novelist Jack Kerouac and adventurer Neal Cassady Arthur

36

Koestler, author of Darkness at Noon and other books, visits Leary and takes psilocybin. He later dismisses the experience as "ersatz mysticism."

January 1961 - Huston Smith's first Psilocybin session

Spring 1961

Gordon Wasson meeting with Richard Evans Schultes meets with Timothy Leary.

March - Richard Alpert's first experience.

March 1961, Tim got a chance to test his utopian vision when he received a letter from Harvard's Department of Legal Medicine. Two officials in the department were looking for help in the psychological rehabilitation of prisoners. At the time, prison work was considered a dead end for psychology research, because criminals never changed and the environment was so grim. Concord Prison Experiment. The project continued for two years, until mid-1963.

Summer 1961

Copenhagen Conference - Leary and the Huxleys at the 14th Annual Congress of Applied Psychology, Copenhagen.

How to Change Behavior paper read.

September 1961

William Burroughs - Leary visits in Tangies and gives him psilocybin. Burroughts then followed Leary back to Harvard. He and Leary present on a panel at the American Psychiatric Association convention in Boston.

Walter Houston Clark, Professor of the Psychology of Religion at Andover Newton Theological Seminary, joins the project as an enthusiastic supporter and advisor.

Professor David McClelland, Director of the Center for Research in Personality where the psilocybin project is housed (and Leary and Alpert's boss) circulates a memo questioning the scientific value of the research, and the societal impact of psychedelic drugs in places like India.

Michael Hollingshead, English freelance researcher and writer, arrives at Tim's house on Grant Avenue. He provides Leary his first LSD session.

November 1961

Important turning point session at Alpert's house in Cambridge, around themes of good and evil, ethics and spiritual leadership. Participants include, besides Leary and Alpert, Ralph Metzner, Michael Kahn, George Litwin and his wife, and Gunther Weil; also, musician Maynard Ferguson and his wife Flo.

December 1961

Michael Hollingshead introduces Timothy Leary to LSD

Winter 1962

Working with Health, Education, and Welfare Dept., Washington D.C.

Spring 1962

Frederick Swain, American Vedantist monk, arrives to visit the Harvard group; introduces group to his Indian guru Gayatri Devi, of the Bengali lineage of Ramakrishna, who headed Vedanta ashrams on the East and

West coasts. Gayatri Devi and Rabbi Zalman Schachter experience psilocybin and become supportive advisors to the project.

At a faculty meeting at the Center for Personality Research, the psilocybin project, and Leary and Alpert personally are vigorously criticized on both scientific and ethical grounds. Social Psychology professor Herbert Kelman is one of the chief critics, as is experimental psychologist Brendan Maher.

Control of the supply of psilocybin is removed from Tim Leary and put in the hands of psychiatrist Dr. Dana Farnsworth, head of the Harvard University Counseling Center. Leary and Alpert are forbidden to give psilocybin to undergraduate students.

The Concord Prison Project is completed; other work with psilocybin comes to an end. The results of that and other studies are written up and published in the psychological and psychiatric journals.

Professor David McClelland, Chair of the Center for Personality Research, tells graduate students on the project, including Metzner, Litwin and Weil, that they will not be able to do their PhD thesis on research with psilocybin.

March 1962 - Good Friday Experiment...

The Harvard Psilocybin Project was officially terminated in the Fall of 1962

The Past and Present

The rediscovery of mind-expanding substances such as psilocybin, mescaline, and LSD in the 1960s was a significant event in the history of human thinking. It challenged the established order of post-World War II culture and threatened the traditional beliefs and understanding of how the world was supposed to operate. The documentation of experimentation with these substances can be traced back to Germany after the war when scientists tested them on prisoners to control their minds. However, the use of these substances by musicians, poets, authors, and intellectuals in North America and Europe brought about a new understanding of the human mind and consciousness. Even though the Harvard Psilocybin Project was shut down, discovering and exploring these substances continued, opening up new avenues of human thinking and understanding. How this will develop depends on many factors which will be considered in the following pages.

Harvard Psilocybin Project 1960-1963

Richard Alpert (AKA RAM DASS) at left with Timothy Leary, 1961

The hunt for the psychedelic origins of Western civilization has to begin with Eleusis. It was one of the oldest religious traditions of Ancient Greece and arguably the most famous. But timing is everything. Forty years ago the Classics establishment was in no position to seriously consider the controversial marriage of the Mysteries and drugs.

Alarm bells were sounding from the towers of academia, as a motley crew of three misfits announced the unthinkable. The code had been cracked. What religious historian Huston Smith called history's "best-kept secret" was a secret no more. After centuries of false leads and dead ends, the unlikely team had finally breached the inner sanctum of the Mysteries of Eleusis. They had discovered what *really* made the Ancient Greeks tick. At long last they had unearthed the true source of our ancestors' poetry and

41

philosophy. Perhaps the hidden inspiration behind the world as we know it. And the answer, they were quite assured, was a magic potion full of psychedelic drugs.

Whenever you accuse the founders of Western civilization of getting stoned out of their minds, and then turning that hallucinatory event into their most cherished religion, a little pushback is to be expected. But the authors of the inflammatory charge couldn't have chosen a worse moment in American history to publish their findings. While most of the excess and hysteria of the 1960s had simmered down, the War on Drugs was just heating up.

Soon, LSD evangelist and countercultural guru, Timothy Leary, was "the most dangerous man in America." (Richard Nixon)

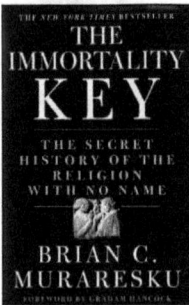

The Germination of the Harvard Psilocybin Program

Tim Leary - 1960

In the winter of 1959, Leary traveled to Florence, Italy with his two children to take a leave of absence after a family tragedy. There he began work on a new manuscript, *The Existential Transaction*, which summarized his ideas for a new psychology. Leary was on sabbatical from the Kaiser Foundation Hospital in Oakland, California. Leary was director of psychology research at the Foundation, and the observations made by the research group were compiled into Leary's magisterial (1957) book Interpersonal Diagnosis of Personality. One of the key ideas of the interpersonal theory was that interpersonal variables are arranged into a circle that later came to be known as the *interpersonal circumplex* which was the early development of interpersonal theory.

In Florance, he met his old pal Frank Barron who was on sabbatical and told Leary about an extraordinary experience he had on a study trip in Mexico. A psychiatrist there had given him a small bag of so-called magic

43

mushrooms which had given him William Blake revelations and transcendental perspectives. He also was given the opportunity in the experience to heal old war trauma.

Leary was fascinated by Barron's extravagant report but also concerned about the professional reputation of his old friend. But Barron had even more to report: Professor David McClelland, Director of the *Center for Personality Research** at Harvard University was also in Florence at that time and, having read Leary's *The Interpersonal Diagnosis of Personality,* might be able to help him find a new job.

2

On Existential Transaction Theory

The Diagnosis of Behavior and the Diagnosis of Experience

Timothy Leary

Timothy Leary's "philosophy" of psychology and understanding originated in his 'Transactional' and 'Existential' revolutionary approach to 'therapy'. He was well known for his groundbreaking 1957 book, *Interpersonal diagnosis of personality; a functional theory and methodology for personality evaluation.* Ronald Press.

44

The book is concerned with interpersonal behavior as observed in the psychotherapeutic setting. The approach might be called dynamic behaviorism, which has two attributes: the impact one person has in interaction with others and the interaction of psychological pressures among different levels of personality. The book is subdivided as follows: Part I. Basic assumptions about personality theory. Part II. Interpersonal dimension of personality—variables, levels, diagnostic categories. Part III. Variability dimension of personality theory and variables. Part IV. Interpersonal diagnosis of personality. Part V. Applications of the interpersonal system. An appendix contains appropriate tables and illustrative materials.

.

David C. McClelland is Professor of Psychology in the Department of Social Relations of Harvard University. He is the author of many books including *The Achieving Society* (available in a Free Press Paperback edition). From 1962 to 1967, Professor McClelland was chairman of the Department of Social Relations of Harvard University.

Professor David McClelland (1917-1998), Director of the *Center for Personality Research* at Harvard University was also in Florence at that time and, having read Leary's *The Interpersonal Diagnosis of Personality*, might be able to help him find a new job. The next day, Leary met McClelland and told him about his next book in which he promoted a new existential understanding of the psychotherapeutic process which took the patient, therapist, their environment, and world views into account as an interactive system. Such a theory was new to McClelland, but he appeared to like Learys plans and vision. After a while, he said: Okay, I am ready to offer you a job. **"You're just what we need to shake things up at Harvard."** Little did McClelland know at the time what he was inviting Harvard University in for.

At 41, David McClelland had already made a name for himself in psychology with his work on "achievement motivation." Described as a "tall, elegant man with a mustache and sharp humor," he was the son of a Methodist minister turned Quaker. McClelland believed that psychoanalysis became popular because it offered a kind of secular comfort for people's existential worries. He would go on to chair Harvard's Department of Social Relations, which was separate from B.F. Skinner's behaviorist-dominated Psychology Department.

Timothy Leary, with his new book in hand, met McClelland over lunch, drinking Chianti on a patio. Leary explained that by "existential," he meant psychologists should work with people in real-life situations, observing behavior in the field rather than applying rigid models. McClelland, impressed by both Leary's work and charm, invited him to Harvard for a year, recalling, "I had admired his work, and we needed strong people for our Ph.D. program."

Timothy Leary

A Biography

Robert Greenfield

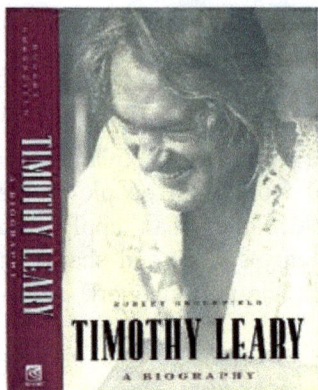

...

GOD AND MAN AT HARVARD

CAMBRIDGE. MASSACHUSETTS.
1958-1963

Leary Meeting McClelland in Florance, Italy in 1959

Frank Barron

Harvard had been denied accreditation for its clinical psychology program and needed top talent like McClelland and Leary to turn things around. McClelland wanted achievers, and Harvard was willing to take risks.

Leary thought of Frank Barron, and McClelland agreed to bring him from Berkeley to Harvard and gave the green light for a one-year psychology research project. It was to start in the fall of 1960, which gave Leary, Barron, and Alpert an entire summer to leisurely develop their plans.

Professor McClelland dropped by my office. There was an opening on the faculty for a one-year appointment. Did I have any suggestions? This was an amazing introduction to power. After six weeks on the job, I was being asked by the Director to recommend staff members for that most coveted post—a Harvard appointment.

49

It was my chance to repay a favor. I suggested Frank Barron and recounted his many virtues. McClelland picked up the phone for a transcontinental conference call with Frank and his boss, Donald McKinnon, Director of the Institute of Personality Assessment and Research (IPAR) at Berkeley. Within a couple of days, it was arranged that Frank would spend the next year as a visiting professor at the Center. I was amazed by the ease with which this transfer was accomplished. Later, I learned there was a continual flow of researchers between the two personality assessment centers. At the top level, everyone seemed to know everyone. I was interested in how these power networks worked, especially when they involved psychology and the government.

Timothy Leary and Richard Alpert, but many other Harvard luminaries such as Richard Schultes, Andrew Weil, David MCelland, Brendan Maher, Herbert Kelman, Nathan Pusey, Dana Farnsworth, Dean John Monro, Herbert Kelman, Henry Beecher, and Harry Murray.

Richard Alpert

One young assistant professor, in particular, stood out: Richard Alpert. He was the son of a wealthy Boston family, had graduated from Stanford University, and had come to Harvard in 1958 as a lecturer in psychology. He was ten years younger than Leary.

Richard Alpert, 1961

The two men were the only faculty members in their department who made themselves available to their students in the evening. Their offices were not far apart, and they soon became friends and decided to start a project together.

Alpert's First Experience

On Saturday night, March 4, 1961, I went to dinner at my parents' house in Newton. I'd just returned to Harvard after my semester at Berkeley. Mother was increasingly frail because of her blood disorder. Dad was struggling with the railroad. A tight-fisted Congress had not approved the federal subsidies he'd lobbied for, and he needed loans and tax relief to stay afloat. In a few short months, the railroad would declare bankruptcy. Dad held on for as long as he could—some said too long.

After dinner, I walked to Tim's house, a three-story mansion perched on a hill only a block away, at 64 Homer Street. He'd rented it from a professor on sabbatical in the Soviet Union and moved in with Susan and Jackie. Newton was just a half-hour drive to Cambridge. The house was grand, with five bedrooms. It had wood-paneled walls, several fireplaces, and bay windows. I was glad it was nearby, because heavy snow had started to fall.

It was my first time seeing Tim since Berkeley, and I was full of anticipation. In the months I'd been gone, Tim had launched a research effort called the Harvard Psilocybin Project with Frank Barron, who was teaching psychology at Harvard that semester. Tim's taste of mushrooms had been so transformative that he'd set out to investigate how psilocybin could be used to broaden human experience. He wanted to find out what kind of people most benefited from it and how its positive effects might be made to last.

Research into hallucinogens was already happening around the country. But many researchers were still using the drugs to mimic psychosis; the CIA-sponsored MK-Ultra project, for example, explored the usefulness of LSD for psychological warfare. Tim was interested in a different line of inquiry. After Mexico, he'd read The Doors of Perception and its sequel, Heaven and Hell, by Aldous Huxley, about the writer's experiences with mescaline, and he'd recognized his own trip in Huxley's words. He wanted to know how these drugs might enhance creativity and meaning.

Tim had spent the fall involving people in the project. When he heard that Huxley was a visiting lecturer at Massachusetts Institute of Technology, just down the road, Tim asked him to be an advisor. Huxley introduced Tim to Huston Smith, a professor of Asian philosophy at MIT who was interested in mystical experiences; his newly published Religions of Man was just becoming popular. Huxley also introduced Tim to Humphry

Osmond, a British scientist who was doing research with psychedelics in Canada, using it in promising ways to cure alcoholism. (They met the same night that John F. Kennedy was voted in as president.) Osmond, in turn, connected Tim to Allen Ginsberg, who had participated in government LSD trials in San Francisco—at the same hospital as Ken Kesey. And Ginsberg introduced Tim to such friends as the writers Jack Kerouac and Robert Lowell and the musicians Dizzy Gillespie, Thelonius Monk, and Maynard Ferguson.

Tim was thrilled. He gave psilocybin to anyone who requested it, in exchange for a detailed report on the experience. In keeping with his existential-transaction ideas, he designed the project with an egalitarian, democratic approach. Rather than the usual clinical, detached method, he wanted both subjects and researchers to participate, taking turns ingesting and observing the effects of psilocybin. He wanted not just psychologists but philosophers, religious types, housewives, cabdrivers, students, and all manner of creatives: musicians, painters, poets, novelists. To avoid the impersonal setting of an office, he invited participants to try the drugs in his own home.

I trusted that Tim had undergone something profound in Mexico. I trusted his intellect. He spoke of the mushroom research as following in the introspective psychology tradition of William James, the father of American psychology. Since I was interested in the internal workings of the mind, this appealed to me. James, as a Harvard professor in the late 1800s, had studied altered states of consciousness using nitrous oxide. Tim was planning on involving our graduate students in the psilocybin research with a new seminar, Experimental Expansion of Consciousness.

Now it was my turn: tonight, I would journey into the unknown. I galumphed into Tim's house, knocking snow from my galoshes.

Sitting in the kitchen was Allen Ginsberg. He was visiting from New York. Tim had not mentioned he'd be there, so 1 was surprised. The last time I'd seen him was at a poetry reading at City Lights Bookstore in San Francisco.

Tim generally disliked homosexuals, but he respected Allen's poetry, which had been recently inspired by LSD and mescaline trips. His book Kaddish and Other Poems was about to come out. Allen and his lover, Peter Orlovsky, had tried psilocybin for the first time at Tim's house, and Allen had become a great friend and supporter of Tim's. Psilocybin was unlike anything Allen had tried, and he thought Tim could lead the country in a new awakening.

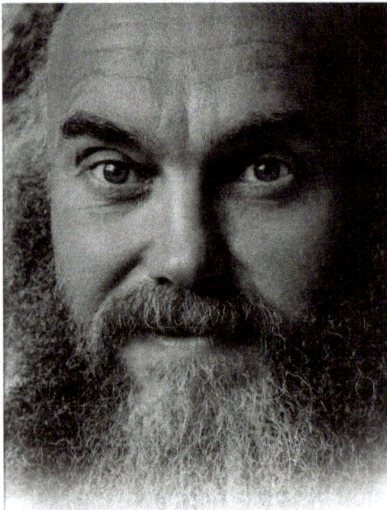

BEING RAM DASS

Foreword by *New York Times* bestselling author Anne Lamott

1996 Video Interview

https://youtu.be/f513g-7P1Ig?si=pS3ooV0XcvTav-I0

The Social Relations Department at Harvard

Harvard University, Department of Social Relations Center for Research in Personality
Morton Prince House, 5 Divinity Avenue

Morton Prince House, where today's Yenching Institute is located, was moved from Divinity Ave on June 12, 1978, adjacent to Hurlburt Hall on 6 Prescott Street, Cambridge.

Leary's office, described as a renovated broom closet, was located in the Center for Personality Research at Harvard University on 5 Divinity Ave. It no longer is there but when you stand on Kirkland Ave and look down Divinity Ave today, you will see to your right Harvard's Psychology building, William James Hall. 5 Divinity Ave was at the tine the Morton Prince House. Morton Prince was one of the first American psychologists to recognize the importance of studying altered states of consciousness. Back in the days when psychologists were gentlemen scholars, he published influential works on unconscious states, coconscious states, and various levels of awareness.

He also founded the Center for Personality Research. Today, his interests in topics like multiple personality, hypnosis, and trances would mark him as a bold and unconventional thinker. It feels fitting that studies on altered states of consciousness would take place in the Morton Prince House.

However, the precedent for psychedelic research at Harvard goes back even further, to the turn of the century, when William James—one of the most revered American psychologists—had mystical experiences with nitrous oxide. He famously claimed to have seen God and even scandalized Boston's elite by hosting drug parties in Back Bay.

Morton Prince

May 2, 1926

HARVARD EXPLAINS PSYCHOLOGY AIMS

Dr. Morton Prince, 72, Says New Science Will Answer the Question, Why? Not What?

FIRST INCUMBENT OF CHAIR

Professor Sees Much Work to Be Done in Abnormal and Dynamic Fields of Science.

Special to The New York Times.

CAMBRIDGE, Mass., May 1.—"By establishing a chair for the teaching of dynamic psychology, Harvard has marked an epoch in the history of "science," declares Dr. Morton Prince, Harvard graduate, and first incumbent of the new chair of dynamic and abnormal psychology announced at the

Asked to explain further the significance of the new professorship, Dr. Prince declared:

"Harvard is the first university in the world to make any such effort toward teaching the vital or dynamic side of psychology. We have been trying for a number of years to induce the universities to enter upon the new field, because of the necessity for the more exact scientific technique of the laboratory, in addition to the inadequate clinical methods on which medical men must rely.

"The psychology which we are instituting at Harvard next year deals with the motivating forces within the personality and the reasons for mental reactions. It answers the question, why? Whereas the present academic psychology deals only with the question, what? We shall go into the subconscious, investigating dreams, inhibitions, repressions, instinctive reactions, and also such abnormal mental phenomena as feeble-mindedness and states of extreme excitement and depression.

After Morton Prince and William James, the legacy of consciousness research at Harvard was carried on by another major figure in psychology:

Harry A. Murray. Murray's work was visionary, full of symbolism like green shirts, white whales, and ideas connecting Freud, Jung, and Melville.

When Harry Murray retired, he moved next door, hanging a whale emblem over the doorway of his new office. David C. McClelland then became the new director of the Center. McClelland, a non-visionary Quaker, embodied the Protestant work ethic—intelligent, tall, puritanical, and driven by external achievement. He had even visited the villa in Cuernavaca the week after Leary's first experience with the magic mushrooms.

The Social Relations Department at Harvard

The Department of Social Relations was created in 1946 by Harvard's social anthropologists, social psychologists, and sociologists.

Towards the end of the 1930's Harvard's Psychology Department found itself divided four to three on every question. The four were E.G. Boring, S.S. Stevens, John G. Beebe-Center, and Karl S. Lashley -- all experimentalists interested in the animal or physiological psychology. By winning every vote they determined the nature of examinations in the field, the selection of graduate students, and all important policies of the department.

The other three were Gordon W. Allport, Robert W. White, and Henry A. Murray, who, by contrast, concerned themselves with personality and its relation to social environment. Frustrated at every point by a department that was both professionally and personally hostile, the minority considered secession.

Theory of Human Behavior

Until 1933, courses in psychology were offered under a Department of Philosophy and Psychology. E. G. Boring, who felt a "mission to rescue Harvard psychology from the philosophers," was largely responsible for the creation of an independent Department of Psychology, and under his direction, psychological studies at Harvard concentrated for a few years on perception and animal learning. But the reorganization of behavioral science disciplines into the *Social Relations Department* restored the traditionally close ties between Psychology and Philosophy.

The Harvard Crimson

The University Daily Est. 1873

Social Relations Dept. Will Study Its Program

Parsons, Two Visiting Teachers Direct Survey into Leading Ideas Behind the Department

NO WRITER ATTRIBUTED

October 18, 1949

Three years after its founding, the Social Relations Department is stopping to analyze what it's teaching.

Professor Talcott Parsons, Chairman of the Department, announced yesterday that he is heading a group which is studying the interrelation of the three divisions of Social Relations: sociology, psychology, and anthropology. This is the first such survey ever made.

Under the auspices of the Carnegie Corporation, the group will work "to improve the theory" which in 1946 led Harvard to form the Department of Social Relations.

"A psychologist," Professor Persons said, "tends to analyze a problem of society in terms of the individual, while a sociologist may view it as a group phenomenon." The program will seek to overcome this friction "resulting from the different intellectual backgrounds of the divisions of Social Relations."

The Psychology Department

An early Harvard Professor's interest in 'substances' and 'consciousness'

William James (1842-1910)

(1872-1907) at Harvard

Established Harvard's Psychology Department

William James, philosopher and psychologist, was instrumental in establishing Harvard's psychology department, which was tied to the department of philosophy at its inception. James himself remained unconvinced that psychology was in fact a distinct discipline, writing in his 1892 survey of the field, Psychology: Briefer Course, "This is no science; it is only the hope of a science" (p. 335). Despite James's skepticism, in the ensuing century, this hope was fully realized in the department he helped to found.

63

Initially trained in painting, James abandoned the arts and enrolled in Harvard in 1861 to study chemistry and anatomy. During an extended stay in Germany after graduating, James developed an interest in studying the mind, as well as the body.. In 1875, James taught one of the university's first courses in psychology, "The Relations between Physiology and Psychology," for which he established the first experimental psychology demonstration laboratory. James oversaw Harvard's first doctorate in psychology, earned by G. Stanley Hall in 1878. Hall noted that James's course was, "up to the present time the only course in the country where students can be made familiar with the methods and results of recent German researches in physiological psychology" (Hall, 1879).

James initiated the Harvard tradition of brain-change research, shocking the academic community with his peyote and nitrous oxide experiments. In 1897, James described his experiments with laughing gas in his essay *The Will to Believe*. His work, *The Varieties of Religious Experience*, made him world famous.

"Some observations on the effects of nitrous-oxide-gas-intoxication which I was prompted to make by reading the pamphlet called The Anaesthetic Revelation and the Gist of Philosophy, by Benjamin Paul Blood, Amsterdam, N. Y., 1874, have made me understand better than ever before... I strongly urge others to repeat the experiment, which with pure gas is short and harmless enough. The effects will of course vary with the individual. Just as they vary in the same individual from time to time; but it is probable that in the former case, as in the latter, a generic resemblance will obtain. With me, as with every other person of whom I have heard, the keynote of the experience is the tremendously exciting sense of an intense metaphysical illumination. Truth lies open to the view in depth beneath depth of almost blinding evidence. The mind sees all the logical relations of being with an apparent subtlety and instantaneity to which its normal consciousness offers no parallel" - The Will to Believe, 1897

History of American Psychology

	Experimental	Clinical	Experiential
1860s	Era of Religion and Moral Philosophy	Era of the Physician and Minister	Literary Psychology of the Transcendentalists
1880s	Physiological Psychology, German psychophysics, and English Mental Testing	The French Experimental Psychology of the Subconscious and Psychical Research	Era of Spiritualism and Mental Healing
1890s	The Functionalism of William James	The Era of Experimental Psychopathology	Christian Science, New Thought and the World Parliament of Religions
1900s	The Era of the ÌSchools" including Gestalt Psychology	The Era of Psychotherapeutics and the Emmanuel Movement Jung precedes Freud	The Depth psychologies of Freud and Jung flourish among the artists and psychics
1910s	Behaviorism takes Control of the academic laboratories	Era of Military psychology and mass Testing	Jung, Freud, and Bergson define popular psychospiritual consciousness; Buchmanites organize into the Oxford Group
1920s	Era of Tests and Measurements and advances in inferential analysis	Tests and Measurements	Era of Psychics, Swamis, Marx, and Radical Sexual Politics
1930s	Age of Theory Begins: Era of Learning Theory versus The Macro-Personality Theorists	Era of Psychoanalytic Ego Psychology Psychosomatic Medicine, and Pastoral Counseling	Radicalization of Social psychology Era of the Surrealists and existentialists; AA is founded
1940s	Era of Military Psychology	Emergence of Scientist-Practitioner Model	Era of Huxley, Merton and Watts begins
1950s	Neo-Behavioristic Era of Modeling begins: Humanistic Psychology emerges as an Academic Endeavor	Humanistic, Existential, and Phenomenological Therapies Dominate Clinical Psychology	Era of Suzuki, Zen and the Beat Generation
1960s	Cognitive Psychology takes over the academic laboratories	Psychedelics, the Community Health Movement, and Client-Centered Therapy challenge psychoanalysis	Human Potential Mvt. Arises, Era of psychedelics begins, Radicalization of depth psychology accelerates. Bodywork and group encounter become the rage
1970s	Cognitive Science expands	Medicalization and over-regulation dominates clinical psychology; Clinicians take control of the American Psychological Assn.	Maslow and Sutich launch Transpersonal Psychology, Absorbs Existential and Humanistic psychology; Gender politics and meditation emerge as new forms of psychotherapy.
1980s	Era of Artificial intelligence, information processing Models; Scientists bolt From APA and form the Amer. Psychological Society	Licensing requirements tighten Psychologist win class action suit Against the MD psychoanalysts; Homosexuality depathologized Behavioral Medicine develops	Shamanism, spirituality and health become linked. Multiculturalism emerges Mind/body medicine develops
1990s	Neuroimaging introduced	Evidenced based practice and psychopharmacology introduced Cognitive therapy colonizes spirituality	Noetic Sciences, Holistic Medicine, Ecopsychology, and entheogens emerge in psychotherapy
2000	Positive Psychology launched and Brain neuroscience expands	Race, Class and Gender become a new focus; Only cognitive and behavioral and psychoanalytic therapies permitted for licensure	Complementary and Alternative therapies, Mind/body medicine, and Socially engaged spirituality emerge

Fig. 1.1 A history of American psychology in three streams

The Lost Potential: How Early Forward-Thinking Academics Could Have Prevented the Failures of the War on Drugs

The early 1960s marked a turning point—not just politically or culturally, but at the deeper edge of what human beings were beginning to uncover about consciousness itself. At Harvard, Timothy Leary and his colleagues were standing right on that edge, exploring psilocybin and other substances, not recklessly, but with a sense of profound potential. They were part of something that might have become one of the most important shifts in how we understand the human psyche. But it didn't happen that way. Instead, the door was slammed shut, and soon after, the so-called "war on drugs" swept the country—not just criminalizing substances, but shutting down the very spirit of inquiry that animated that moment.

It's tempting to think of this early psychedelic research as isolated to Harvard, but in truth, there were small centers of experimentation springing up all over. Progressive thinkers—therapists, teachers, spiritual explorers— were beginning to realize these substances weren't just drugs; they were tools, or at least doorways, to something deeper. These weren't wild-eyed idealists. Many were disciplined thinkers, academically trained, unafraid to challenge convention, and deeply attuned to the complexity of what it means to be human.

Among them, though not always named in this history, was Gordon Allport—one of Harvard's most influential psychologists. Allport had spent decades shaping the field of personality psychology, emphasizing individuality, the inward life, and even the possibility of self-transcendence. His work aligned closely with what Leary and others were aiming for: understanding how these substances could catalyze insight, empathy, even creative and emotional breakthroughs. But Allport wasn't brought into the inner circle of public discourse around psychedelics. And that absence—his and others'—left Leary and his team exposed to a wave of media frenzy, bureaucratic resistance, and cultural panic.

What followed wasn't just a policy shift. It was a cultural shutdown. The narrative was hijacked—no longer about inquiry or possibility, but about danger and deviance. The research wasn't questioned on scientific grounds; it was discarded wholesale under the banner of protecting the youth. A moral crusade replaced a scientific dialogue, and in doing so, it strangled a field that had only just begun to emerge.

The cost of that reactionary turn was—and still is—staggering. The war on drugs didn't just criminalize substances; it criminalized curiosity. It made pariahs of researchers, halted promising studies, and blocked what might have become a revolution in mental health, creativity, and human development. In its place, fear took root. Not reasoned caution, but institutionalized fear—fear of the unknown, fear of loss of control, fear of letting the soul have its say.

Had voices like Allport's been welcomed into the conversation—measured, informed, and grounded—there's every reason to believe the story could have unfolded differently. Leary may have had allies not only in the academy but also among policymakers, educators, and even the public. The research might have continued—not in chaos or rebellion, but in a disciplined, human way. And we might be living now in a culture that embraced the mysteries of the mind rather than recoiling from them.

But that's not what happened. And so we look back—not with nostalgia, but with the sober recognition that an opportunity was lost. One that might still be recovered, but only if we learn from what was pushed aside.

THE USE OF PERSONAL DOCUMENTS IN PSYCHOLOGICAL SCIENCE

Prepared for the Committee on Appraisal of Research

BY

GORDON W. ALLPORT

The publication of Gordon Allport's, 1942 monograph, The Use of Personal Documents in Psychological Science (UPD), was a crucial landmark, one which served as a "prophetic" call for proper qualitative methodology that was justifiably scientific. "[Allport] asserted that the study of personal documents is indispensible to knowledge of subjective personal life and provides scientific psychology with a touchstone of reality by means of a genuine scientific method" - Fred Wertz, (Professor, Fordham University)

Gordon Allport and the Turn Toward Subjective Understanding in Psychology

In the early 20th century, psychology in America was dominated by behaviorism and experimentalism—fields that sought to model the mind according to the standards of objective science, often at the expense of the very subjectivity they purported to study. Within this climate, Gordon W. Allport emerged as a quiet but powerful revolutionary. His 1941 monograph, *The Use of Personal Documents in Psychological Science*, written while teaching at Harvard University, marked a turning point in how the human psyche could be approached, understood, and honored.

In the preface to his work, Allport reflects on how the social upheavals of the Depression and World War II brought renewed attention to the individual—the common person's fears, hopes, struggles, and inner life. Popular culture began to reflect this shift with candid interviews, autobiographies, and the rise of the documentary. Allport saw that psychology, too, had to follow this tide—not by abandoning rigor, but by broadening the field's definition of valid data to include the subjective, the personal, and the confessional.

His argument centered on the "personal document": first-person, self-revealing records such as diaries, letters, autobiographies, and spontaneous verbal accounts. These materials, Allport insisted, offer an irreplaceable window into the structure and dynamics of the human mind as it is actually lived. Though many in the scientific community dismissed such sources as too singular, unreliable, or unreplicable, Allport emphasized that these very features made them *more* psychologically real—not less.

Allport was not naïve about the limitations of subjective material. In fact, he constructed a detailed analytic framework to assess personal documents with methodological rigor.

Working with Harvard students, and with the support of the Social Science Research Council, Allport's seminar-based research became a formative statement on psychology's evolving identity. His influence seeded later developments in humanistic psychology, narrative psychology, and qualitative methods—fields that continue to explore the nuanced interplay of person, story, and meaning.

Allport's work signaled that the subjective dimension of human life is not a flaw in the data, but its heart. In this way, he helped reorient psychology at Harvard and beyond—away from a narrow conception of objectivity and toward a more integrative science of persons.

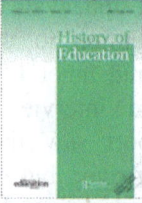

History of Education

Journal of the History of Education Society

R Routledge
Taylor & Francis Group

ISSN: 0046-760X (Print) 1464-5130 (Online) Journal homepage: https://www.tandfonline.com/loi/thed20

From recreational to functional drug use: the evolution of drugs in American higher education, 1960–2014

Ross D. Aikins

This paper traces substance use and research trends in American higher education over the past half-century, divided into three eras defined by their disparate approaches to drug policy and public health. Contextualised by historic events, shifting policies and epidemiological data, this multi-disciplinary analysis contends that functional, academically oriented drug use is likely to continue rising on US campuses, while recreational drug use will evolve and persist. As history provides a useful lens for understanding the involvement of academe in the first era of drug concern in America, ongoing innovations in medical and social science may be instructive to help ensure that institutions respond judiciously in the present era of new drug synthesis and drug policy recession.

Perception and Perspective

The project not only went against the grain of academic research, but it was also fundamentally a threat to perception and the psychology of the individual.

Las Meninas ('The Ladies-in-waiting' - *las me'ninas*), 1656, Diego Velázquez, Spanish Baroque.

1957, Las Meninas, Pablo Picasso - variations of Diego Velazquez's painting. Cubism

Humanists vs Experimentalist

"You're just what we need to shake things up at Harvard"

David McClelland to Timothy Leary, 1959

The Department of Psychology at Harvard continued to be divided between its experimentalists, who dominated the department, and its social-clinical wing, which in the 1960s resided in Social Relations.

The problem, University President Dean Pusey thought, was "[h]ow to build back a strong unified department of psychology?" That would not be easy. Social psychologist David McClelland, who became the chair of Social Relations in 1962, complained of how hard it was to deal with Stanley Smith Stevens, the director of the Psychological Laboratory. Stevens was a severe, traditional experimentalist, uninterested in undergraduates. But the standing of Harvard's experimental psychologists was not to be sneezed at. Stevens's colleague Georg von Bekesy, won a Nobel Prize in Medicine in 1961 for his work on the inner ear. And the Psychological Lab was the home of the brilliant (and controversial) B. F. Skinner's work on conditioning. The problem required breaking through into new territory.

The self-appointed scientists and the academics were skeptical and irritated. They sensed what I was up to and knew that my charisma and enthusiasm could make it work.

The psychedelic sages also murmured against the research plan. It was too public, too superficial, too easy.

The psychedelic underground. The handful of Americans who knew where it was at most of them long-time students of oriental philosophy and mystic experiences.

72

"When you can measure what you are speaking about and express it in numbers, you know something about it, when you cannot express it in numbers, your knowledge is of a meager and unsatisfactory kind."

Henry K. Beecher, Harvard University Medical School, a staunch critic of the Psilocybin Project, quoting Lord Kelvin-William Thomson

Harvard Medical School, under the direction of Henry Beecher, was experimenting with LSD as early as 1954.

PSYCHOTOMIMETIC DRUGS

HENRY K. BEECHER, M.D.
BOSTON, MASS.

From The Anesthesia Laboratory of the Harvard Medical School at the Massachusetts General Hospital

(Received for publication April 26, 1958.)

PART I: BACKGROUND

FOREWORD

MODERN interest in the psychotomimetic drugs goes back more than a hundred years[79] and active experimentation more than 75 years.[64,101] In this time a vast literature has accumulated. It is not the intention of the reviewer to attempt to describe all of this. It is important, then, that present purposes be explicitly stated: (a) to cover originally observed facts and statements of concepts; (b) to present current views concerning the effects, the uses, the difficulties, and the possibilities inherent in the psychotomimetic drugs, especially as they have been studied in man; (c) in all of this, to emphasize the well-designed study when encountered—and what seem to be the requirements for such study— and to give suitable emphasis to *quantitative* data wherever it can be found. The reviewer holds with Lord Kelvin that ". . . when you can measure what you are speaking about, and express it in numbers, you know something about it . . . when you cannot express it in numbers, your knowledge is of a meager and unsatisfactory kind; it may be the beginning of knowledge, but you have scarcely, in your thoughts, advanced to the stage of *Science* . . . ." A final purpose is to arrive at some general conclusions concerning work in this field.

Interdisciplinary Education

The founding of *Social Relations* was distinguished by a vigorous enthusiasm for an experiment in interdisciplinary education, and the vision which guided the planners of the new department was every bit as exciting as that which inspired their contemporaries, the designers of Harvard's General Education program. In addition to their **goal of drafting a general theory of human behavior**, the social relationists also set out to broaden the intellectual base of the behavioral sciences.

The founders of the Department were eminently qualified for these undertakings: Henry Murray, trained in medicine and psychoanalysis, was also an eminent Melville scholar; Clyde Kluckhohn had studied classics before he took up cultural anthropology; Gordon Allport traced his roots at Harvard back to the old Department of Social Ethics; and Talcott Parsons' interests extended beyond orthodox sociology to economics and politics.

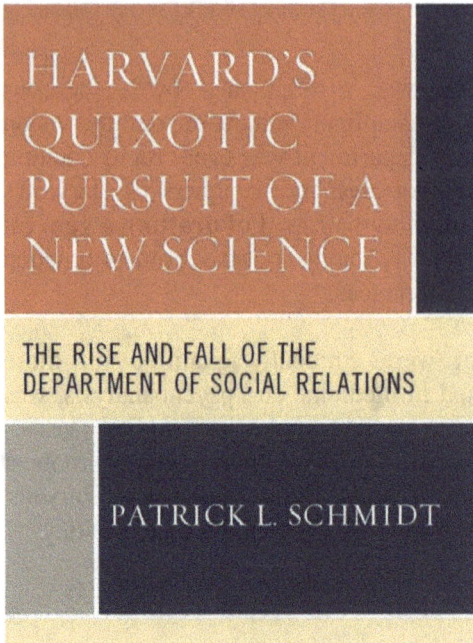

Harvard's Quixotic Pursuit of a New Science (The Rise and Fall of the Department of Social Relations), Patrick L. Schmidt. In Harvard's Quixotic Pursuit of a New Science, Schmidt tells the little-known story of how some of the most renowned social scientists of the twentieth century struggled to elevate their emerging disciplines of cultural anthropology, sociology, and social and clinical psychology. Scorned and marginalized in their respective departments in the 1930s for pursuing the controversial theories of Freud and Jung, they persuaded Harvard to establish a new department, promising to create an interdisciplinary science that would surpass in importance Harvard's "big three" disciplines of economics, government, and history.

Patrick L. Schmidt is an attorney in Washington, D.C. He received a BA, magna cum laude, from Harvard College, a JD from Georgetown University, and an MIPP from the Johns Hopkins University School of Advanced International Studies. He first examined the history of the Department of Social Relations in his undergraduate honors thesis at Harvard, meaning that he has lived with and examined this story for many years now. (https://patrickschmidtauthor.com/)

America Becomes Aware of 'Magic Mushrooms'

Back in 1955, an American mycologist and researcher named R. Gordon Wasson made an exciting discovery in Oaxaca, Mexico. Wasson, who also happened to be the vice president of J.P. Morgan, came across a type of mushroom with some pretty powerful and unusual effects. His curiosity got the best of him, so he invited a fellow mycologist, Professor Roger Heim, who was the Director of the National Museum of Natural History in Paris, to come along and check things out.

In 1956, Heim joined Wasson in Oaxaca, where they gathered some of these fascinating mushrooms. Heim took them back to his lab in Paris, where he successfully identified the mushrooms and even managed to grow cultures of them. He named the species Psilocybe Mexicana Heim. Heim then sent a sample over to the Sandoz Research Laboratories in Switzerland to dive deeper into its chemistry.

Fast forward to 1957, when Albert Hofmann—yes, the same guy who discovered LSD—coined the term "psilocybin." It's the name of the active compound he isolated from those Psilocybe Mexicana mushrooms. It turns out that the Psilocybe genus includes over 100 species of mushrooms worldwide, all containing psilocybin. After isolating the molecule, Hofmann and his team managed to synthesize it in crystalline form in 1958.

For a while in the 1960s, Sandoz Laboratories even sold a synthetic version under the name Indocybin.

Life Magazine, 1957 - Gordon Wasson

In the May 13, 1957 issue of Life magazine, R. Gordon Wasson revealed the discovery of the sacred mushroom cult of Mexico. His article, "Seeking the Magic Mushroom," depicted several species of hallucinogenic mushrooms, and described the modern cult and its history. The title, chosen by the editors of Life, caught the popular fancy, and psilocybin fungi were known thenceforth as 'magic mushrooms.' Wasson timed the publication of his article to coincide with the release of Mushrooms, Russia, and History, which he co-authored with his wife Valentina *A BRIEF HISTORY OF HALLUCINOGENIC MUSHROOMS*. This magnificent two-volume limited edition of 512 copies detailed 30 years of study of the field the Wassons named 'ethnomycology.'

Starting with an arduous study of European mushroom names, the Wassons' astonishing odyssey had led them to the rediscovery of the sacred mushrooms of Mexico.

In this remarkable book, they presented their initial observations on the modern cult of *teonandcatl*, and included a thorough review of its history. With precision and perspicacity, in moving language, Gordon Wasson reverently described the effects of the mushrooms and the significance of his discovery. As befits a great book, Mushrooms, Russia and History became an instant classic, and has sold for up to $1750 at auction.

The Wassons had found the last dying remains of a once mighty cult. In only a few remote areas of Mexico did the mushrooms continue to hold sway over the Indians. In every case where ritual use of the mushrooms was encountered, the beliefs surrounding the cult were mingled inextricably with Christian concepts. The mushrooms were personified as Jesus, and rites were celebrated before crude wooden altars bearing icons representing the baptism in J*ordan and Santo Nino de Atocha* (a Catholic conception of the young Jesus).

Soon after the publication of the Life article, outsiders, in search of the mushroom experience, began to make the pilgrimage to Huautla de Jimenez. Maria Sabina became the high priestess of a modern mushroom cult born, like the Phoenix, from the ashes of its predecessor (11,48). In Huautla and other villages, the mushrooms were profaned, reduced merely to articles of the tourist trade. Postcards depicting mushrooms, clothes embroidered with mushroom motifs, and the mushrooms themselves were widely and conspicuously sold (46,47). The transformation of the mushrooms to articles of commerce virtually destroyed the remains of the

81

ancient cult. Self-styled shamans staged spurious mushroom ceremonies for the benefit of the tourists. Maria Sabina herself pronounced a fitting epitaph to the secret cult she had divulged to the world: "Before Wasson, I felt that the mushrooms exalted me. Now I no longer feel this .... From the moment the strangers arrived ... the mushrooms lost their purity. They lost their power, they decomposed. From that moment on they no longer worked."

"There is a world beyond ours, a world that is far away, nearby, and invisible. And there is where God lives, where the dead live, the spirits and the saints, a world where everything has already happened, and everything is known. That world talks. It has a language of its own. I report what it says. The sacred mushroom takes me by the hand and brings me to the world where everything is known. It is they, the sacred mushrooms, that speak in a way I can understand. I ask them and they answer me. When I return from the trip that I have taken with them, I tell what they have told me and what they have shown me."

Maria Sabina

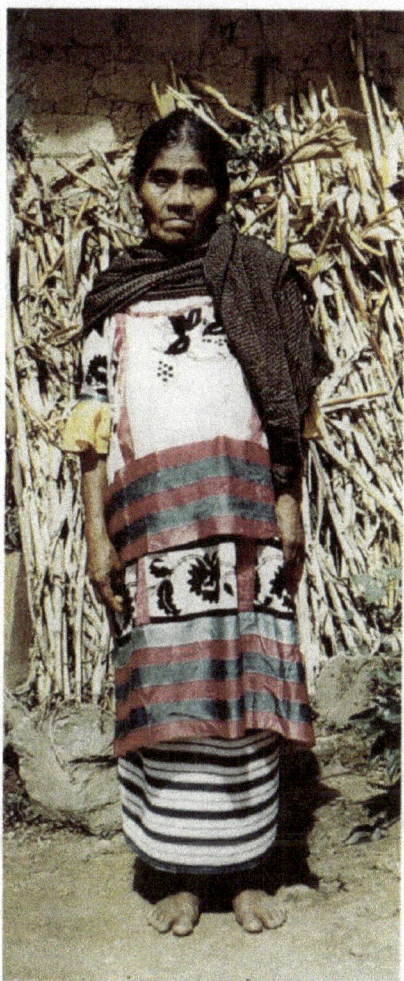

Above: Albert Hofmann visited the shaman María Sabina in 1962 and took many portraits of her.

Thus does the famous Mazatec shaman Maria Sabina reverently describe the god-given powers of the intoxicating mushrooms that she uses in her ceremony, which has come down from ages past.

Taken from: TEONANACATL - HALLUCINOGENIC MUSHROOMS OF NORTH AMERICA. Edited by Jonathan Ott and Jeremy Bigwood.

The article

It was only a few years later did the American public learned of the revelation of the sacred mushroom ceremony when Gordon Wasson and photographer Allan Richardson revealed a June 1955 *velada* or sacred mushroom ceremony led by Maria Sabina in a Life magazine article in 1957. They had participated in the ritual themselves. Mr. Wasson was inspired by the fantastic effects and concluded that humans exploring foods in ancient times would have encountered the mushrooms and that the impact "could only have been profound, a detonator to new ideas." He wrote that when Cortez conquered Mexico, his followers noticed the Aztecs eating mushrooms in a religious setting and calling them God's flesh or teonanacatl. He described art works in the region going back to a thousand years earlier, such as mushroom stones in Guatemala. In addition to Central American mushroom stones 1000 years old, the ceremonial use of psilocybin mushrooms is apparently depicted on the Aztec Prince of flowers, a seated divine male figure, carved in stone during the 1500s, with stylized mushrooms on its body, along with tobacco, *ololiuqui*, the hallucinogenic morning glory flower.

Gordon and Valentina Wasson continued to travel to Mexico, and in 1956, Roger Heim, the director of the French Museum of Natural History and a leading researcher on mycology, traveled with them. After Tina Wasson's death in 1958, Dr. Heim returned with Gordon Wasson in 1959 and 1961, and in 1962, Albert Hofmann and his wife Anita traveled there. A 1958 recording with translations from the Mazatec language, released as Maria Sabina and her Mazatec Mushroom Velada, was his proudest accomplishment among many discoveries. An excellent source about these discoveries is The Sacred Mushroom Seeker, (1990), a series of essays about Gordon Wasson edited by Thomas Redlinger.

TEXT CONTINUED ON PAGE 100

The Hallucinogenic Fungi Of Mexico

An Inquiry Into The Origins of The Religious Idea Among Primitive Peoples

R. Gordon Wasson

In the fall of 1952 we learned that the 16th century writers, describing the Indian cultures of Mexico, had recorded that certain mushrooms played a divinatory role in the religion of the natives. Simultaneously we learned that certain pre-Columbian stone artifacts resembling mushrooms, most of them roughly a foot high, had been turning up, usually in the highlands of Guatemala, in increasing numbers. For want of a better name, the archeologists called them "mushroom stones," but not one archeologist had linked them with mushrooms or with the rites described by the 16th century writers in neighboring Mexico. They were an enigma, and "mushroom stone" was merely a term of convenience. Some of these stone carvings carried an effigy on the stipe, either a human face or an animal, and all of them were very like mushrooms. Like the child in the Emperor's New Clothes, we spoke up, declaring that the so-called "mushroom stones" really represented mushrooms, and that they were the symbol of a religion, like the Cross in the Christian religion, or the Star of Judea, or the Crescent of the Moslems. If we are right—and little by little the accumulating evidence seems to be in our favor—then this Middle American cult of a divine mushroom, this cult of "God's flesh" as the Indians in pre-Columbian times called it, can be traced back to about B.C. 1500, in what we call the Early Pre-classic period, the earliest period in which man was in sufficient command of his technique to be able to carve stone. Thus we find a mushroom in the center of the cult with perhaps the oldest continuous history in the world. These oldest mushroom stones are technically and stylistically among the finest that we have, evidence of a flourishing rite at the time they were made. Earlier still, it is tempting to imagine countless generations of wooden effigies, mushroomic symbols of the cult, that have long since turned to dust. Is not mycology, which someone has called the step-child of the sciences, acquiring a wholly new and unexpected dimension? Religion has always been at the core of man's highest faculties and cultural achievements, and therefore I ask you now to contemplate our lowly mushroom—what patents of ancient lineage and nobility are coming its way!

This paper was first given as the Annual Lecture of the Mycological Society of America, Stillwater, Oklahoma, 1960, and later published in the Botanical Museum Leaflets, Harvard University, 1961, **Gordon Wasson**

See paper: https://beezone.com/hallucinogenic-fungi-of-mexico

The Botony Connection at Harvard

Botany, Biology, Psychology, and Consciousness

Brian D. Farrell

Monique and Philip Lehner Professor for the Study of Latin America
Professor of Biology
Curator of Entomology in the Museum of Comparative Zoology

Faculty Support: Amie Jones

Much of our work tests hypotheses concerning the influence of spatial and temporal variation in the availability of habitats or other resources on speciation and the rate of evolution of interspecific interactions. Our data are largely phylogenetic, based on variation in DNA sequences and morphological characters, and our studies vary in focus from principally ecological dimensions of resource use to emphasis on biogeographic or paleontological dimensions. Our general goal to understand the interplay of adaptation and historical contingency in ecological and taxonomic diversification, as well as the marks of evolutionary history on community structure. The context of nearly all of our studies is the interaction between insects and plants, ecological associates whose diversity and abundance make them the principal denizens of the terrestrial earth.

89

Brian D. Farrell, Director, David Rockefeller Center for Latin American Studies; Professor of Biology, Department of Organismic and Evolutionary Biology, Harvard University

"I wish to connect William James' (father of psychology) perspective on religion and consciousness with the work of another Harvard professor concerned with the particulars of human spiritual life, Richard Evans Schultes, known as the father of ethno-botany."

Biology of Consciousness - Brian Farrell ReVista

HARVARD REVIEW OF LATIN AMERICA

The Biology of Consciousness

> *"I am neither a theologian, nor a scholar learned in the history of religions,nor ananthropologist.*

Psychology is the only branch of learning in which I am particularly versed. To the psychologist the religious propensities of man must be at least as interesting as any other of the facts pertaining to his mental constitution. It would seem, therefore, that, as a psychologist, the natural thing for me would be to invite you to a descriptive survey of those religious propensities." —Williams James *(On the Varieties of Religious Experience.* Longmans, Green, & Co. 1902).

Substitute the word biology for psychology, and you'd have my consideration of consciousness—my own curiosity in writing about that subject parallels that of James about religion. His words, written more than a hundred years ago, have a sounding resonance with what and how I—as a biologist—have come to understand the realms of consciousness: *"In my belief that a large acquaintance with particulars often makes us wiser than the possession of abstract formulas, however deep... "* Therefore, in this work at least, William James, widely regarded as the father of American

90

psychology, was what some would today call a phenomenologist (a concern with observations, case studies and the like that may be contrasted with purely theoretical approaches).

Trained in medicine, William James first taught physiology at Harvard and had absorbed Darwin's view of evolution and in particular, the observation that ubiquitous random variation sometimes leads to evolutionary innovations. James was a scientist but did not favor what he termed *scientism*—the position of some fellow intellectuals who demurred from discussing certain subjects (presumably such as religion) as being outside their discipline, and unscientific (he named H. G. Wells and Bernard Shaw, among others). James thought broadly, and yet saw that all human behaviors are probably ultimately grounded in biology.

In offering some biological particulars, I wish to connect William James' perspective on religion and consciousness with the work of another Harvard professor concerned with the particulars of human spiritual life, Richard Evans Schultes, known as the father of ethno-botany.

His lifelong work was documenting the indigenous uses of plants and fungi throughout the Americas, including in religious rituals. He began his Harvard career with an undergraduate senior thesis on the Kiowa peyote rituals in the southwestern United States, moved on in later years to identifying the species termed Ololiuqui (morning glory seeds containing LSD) and Teonanacatl (*Psilocybe* mushrooms) by the ancient Aztecs in Mexico, using images depicted in the few remaining Aztec codices, and finally, spent many years exploring the Amazon forests of Colombia and beyond, with shamans documenting ayahuasca rituals, and collecting tens of thousands of plant specimens now deposited in the Harvard University Herbaria.

From William James to Richard Schultes
by Brian D. Farrell | Sep 26, 2016

91

Harvard's Botany Connection

Mushrooms and the University

Harvard University Herbaria

Richard Evans Schultes

Schultes at Chiribiquete
Photograph courtesy of the Schultes Family and the Amazon Conservation team

BOTANICAL MUSEUM LEAFLETS
HARVARD UNIVERSITY

Cambridge, Massachusetts, February 21, 1939   Vol. 7, No. 3

PLANTAE MEXICANAE II
BY
Richard Evans Schultes

THE IDENTIFICATION OF TEONANACATL,
A NARCOTIC BASIDIOMYCETE OF THE AZTECS

I. Introduction

Investigations dealing with the vegetable narcotics, intoxicants, and poisons used by primitive peoples comprise studies which involve some of the most fundamental culture-traits. The narcotic plants of the New World especially are attracting popular attention while stimulating scientific interest. In this connection, a large ethnobotanical and ethnopharmacological literature is being developed. A recent anthropological study (13) has briefly summarized some of the information concerning the primitive uses of a number of narcotics and has emphasized the importance to theoretical anthropology of correctly identified and thoroughly investigated ethnobotanical material. Indeed, this summary and other recent papers have clearly emphasized the need, as well as the desirability, of further botanical and ethnological investigations of plant narcotics, their uses, and their significance.

The plant narcotics of Mexico are of unique interest

Botanical Museum Leaflets, Harvard University

Vol. 7, No. 3 (February 21, 1939), pp. 37-56 (19 pages)

Published By: Harvard University Herbaria

Richard Schultes with a Shaman examining plant materials in the Colombian Amazon. Photo courtesy of Harvard College and Fellows.

The story of Harvard's involvement with psychedelic research, particularly with sacred mushrooms, traces its roots well before the famous Harvard Psilocybin Project of the 1960s, involving Timothy Leary and Richard Alpert (later known as Ram Dass). Long before Leary and Alpert began their experiments, the Harvard Botany Department played a critical role in ethnobotany and the study of psychoactive plants, thanks in large part to Richard Evans Schultes.

Schultes, who entered Harvard as an undergraduate in 1933 and later became a professor in 1953, is widely considered the father of modern ethnobotany. His work focused on indigenous knowledge of medicinal and psychoactive plants in the Amazon rainforest, and he became a pioneer in the academic study of these substances. Schultes was particularly interested in how indigenous peoples used plants in rituals and healing practices, with a significant portion of his research centering on the use of psychoactive substances like ayahuasca and the sacred mushroom, Psilocybe mexicana.

Schultes' connection to the sacred mushroom predates the widespread attention to psychedelics in Western culture. In the early 20th century, knowledge of hallucinogenic mushrooms was largely limited to indigenous communities in Mesoamerica. One key figure in the rediscovery of this knowledge was R. Gordon Wasson, a banker-turned-mycologist who famously participated in a mushroom ceremony in Mexico in 1955 and wrote about it in Life magazine in 1957. Schultes, however, had already laid the scientific groundwork by the time Wasson published his now-famous article.

Schultes' early research into psychoactive plants, including Psilocybe species, played a significant role in validating the ethnobotanical and pharmacological importance of these substances. His detailed fieldwork among indigenous peoples of the Amazon and Mexico, where he documented the use of psychoactive plants in shamanic rituals, helped bridge the gap between indigenous knowledge and Western science.

Thus, the "earlier story" of Harvard and the sacred mushroom begins with Schultes and his quiet yet profound academic contributions to the study of ethnobotany, which laid the groundwork for later figures, such as Wasson, Leary, and Alpert, who would bring these substances to the forefront of

Western consciousness. Schultes' work represents a more traditional, scientifically grounded approach to understanding these plants, distinct from the more controversial experimentation with psychedelics that came later.

Wade Davis on Richard Evans Schultes

https://www.youtube.com/watch?v=5wI4-Cqkvwg

The Amazonian Travels of Richard Evans Schultes

The one on the right has a Harvard degree.

Public Lecture by Mark Plotkin, Co-Founder and President of the Amazon Conservation Team

https://www.youtube.com/watch?v=91X0UMLjn04

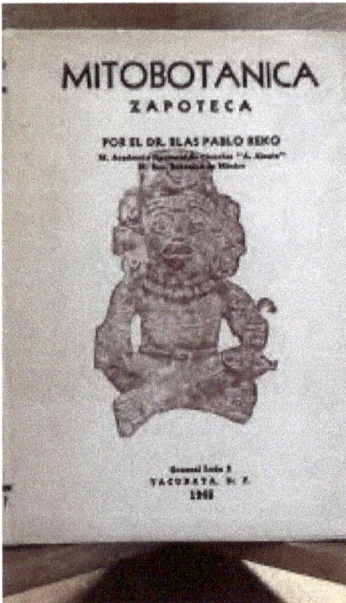

Blas Pablo Reko's collaboration with Richard Evans Schultes in the 1930s marked a pivotal moment in the rediscovery of the ceremonial use of hallucinogenic mushrooms in Mesoamerica. During his research in Mexico, Reko reported evidence of mushroom use in religious ceremonies among the indigenous peoples of Oaxaca. This discovery piqued the interest of the scientific community and led to a series of expeditions to gather and study the mushrooms.

98

In 1938, Reko traveled to Oaxaca with Schultes, then a young Harvard ethnobotanist, to collect samples of these sacred mushrooms. The samples they gathered were sent to Harvard University for analysis. Their findings attracted the attention of other researchers, including North American anthropologist Jean Bassett Johnson. Intrigued by the reports of Mazatec mushroom ceremonies, Johnson traveled to Oaxaca the following year, in 1939, to observe the ceremonies firsthand. He became the first documented Western scientist to witness a traditional mushroom ceremony, an event that would later inspire significant interest in the cultural and spiritual use of psychoactive fungi in the West.

In the 1940s, Rolf Singer, a renowned mycologist, studied the mushroom samples collected by Schultes and identified some of them as Psilocybe cubensis, which he classified as narcotic mushrooms. This identification was a key step in linking these mushrooms to their psychoactive properties, as it allowed Western scientists to better understand their biological and chemical makeup.

Schultes' work in Mexico continued to inspire other researchers and adventurers interested in the ritual use of psychoactive mushrooms. Among them were Robert Gordon Wasson, a wealthy U.S. banker, and his wife Valentina Pavlovna. Inspired by Schultes' research and his exploration of indigenous knowledge, the Wassons traveled to Mexico in 1952 with the goal of gaining a deeper understanding of how Psilocybe mushrooms were used in Mazatec culture. Their journey ultimately led to Wasson's famous 1957 Life magazine article, which introduced the sacred mushrooms and their ceremonial use to a broader Western audience.

The Messiah

Messiah

"The promised deliverer of the Jewish nation prophesied in the Hebrew Bible"

"Jesus regarded by Christians as the Messiah of the Hebrew prophecies and the savior of humankind"

"A leader or savior of a particular group or cause"

"Anointed - Consecrated (made sacred by God) - 'Called to lead'"

DR TIMOTHY LEARY PHD

The Return to Harvard and The Climate of the Times

Fall Semester, 1960

September - December

We members of the Harvard Center for Personality Research, presumably an advanced psychology think tank, were completely unaware that the second American Civil War was about to explode, that the old control society was about to collide with the new communication culture. Yet I had been unwittingly prepared—being genetically designed, scientifically trained, temperamentally ready, and perfectly located—to surf this wave of change.

Flashbacks, Notes on chapter 2, pp. 387-388.

"This is the Space Age, and we are Here to Go"

Foreword to High Priest - Allen Ginsberg

I did not wander barefoot forth from Mexico preaching the word. I flew back to Harvard University and started a research project. The strategy was to provide religious experiences and then scientifically measure the overt benefit.

Timothy Leary, Flashbacks

Let the Games Begin

Leary arrives at Harvard in January 1960

Having come to Cambridge to resurrect his failing career, Tim did everything he could to get off to "a fast start on the Harvard academic track." When he was offered a suite of offices on the third floor of the Center for Personality Research, a "Puritan-style frame building located, prophetically enough, at 5 Divinity Avenue," Tim instead chose a small typist's office close to the entrance to the building because he wanted to be "near the center of the action."

Professor McClelland dropped by my office. There was an opening on the faculty for a one-year appointment. Did I have any suggestions? This was an amazing introduction to power. After six weeks on the job, I was being asked by the Director to recommend staff members for that most coveted post—a Harvard appointment.

It was my chance to repay a favor. I suggested Frank Barron and recounted his many virtues. McClelland picked up the phone for a transcontinental conference call with Frank and his boss, Donald McKinnon, Director of the Institute of Personality Assessment and
Research (IPAR) at Berkeley.

Within a couple of days it was arranged that Frank would spend the next year as a visiting professor at the Center. I was amazed by the ease with which this transfer was accomplished. Later I learned there was a continual flow of researchers between the two personality assessment centers. At the top level everyone seemed to know everyone. I was interested in how these power networks worked, especially when they involved psychology and the government.

Leary's First Semester Meets and Befriends Richard Alpert

Timothy Leary's approach to psychology was unconventional from the start. Instead of sending his graduate students to work in Freudian-oriented clinics and hospitals, where they would learn sterile and ineffective tests like the Rorschach Ink Blots, he urged them to engage with real-world problems. Leary encouraged his students to tackle issues in places like skid rows, ghetto community centers, Catholic orphanages, marriage clinics, and jails. His aim was to immerse them in environments that exposed them to the human condition in its rawest forms.

Leading by example, Leary accompanied his students on their fieldwork. They interviewed junkies, street cops, and social workers, gaining firsthand insight into the struggles faced by society's marginalized. Leary also facilitated meetings with prominent figures such as Bill Wilson, the founder of Alcoholics Anonymous, and Charles Dederich, the founder of Synanon, a therapeutic community for substance abusers. His efforts were rooted in a desire to be at the forefront of the humanistic psychology movement, which sought a more holistic understanding of the human experience.

Leary's commitment to innovation was evident in his writings, where he expressed his dissatisfaction with the existing psychological frameworks.

"We operate with too little information about ourselves and the other guy," he later reflected. "I don't have any theory about new variables in psychology, no new words or language. I am simply trying to develop new ways of feeding back to human beings what they are doing and the noises they are making." This forward-thinking approach, however, was not well-received by everyone at Harvard, where he was a faculty member.

By May 1960, Leary had begun to frustrate the administration at Harvard. David McClelland, his supervisor, penned a two-page letter on May 3rd addressing concerns about Leary's conduct both in and out of the classroom. Although McClelland expressed sympathy for Leary's goals, he highlighted three key issues: vagueness, over-generalization, and a disregard for scientific evidence. McClelland's critique was direct: "At times you seem very cavalier on this issue—as if to say that the rules of evidence that science has worked out are all nonsense—that the ravings of a madman or an idiot are as valuable as the careful investigations of a psychologist."

It was around this time that Leary met and befriended Richard Alpert, an assistant professor who worked down the hall from him at the Center for Personality Research. The two men, the only faculty members who held office hours in the evening, would go on to have a profound influence on each other's work.

Once the academic year ended, Leary set off for Mexico for the fourth consecutive summer. He planned to work on his unfinished book, but his time in Mexico would have an even greater impact on his life and career. During his stay, he experienced a profound spiritual awakening. As he later recounted, "Three years ago, on a sunny afternoon in the garden of a Cuernavaca villa, I ate seven of the so-called 'sacred mushrooms'... During the next five hours, I was whirled through an experience which... was above all and without question the deepest religious experience of my life."

105

This encounter with psilocybin mushrooms left him feeling exhilarated, convinced that he had awakened from "a long ontological sleep."

Leary's transformative experience in Mexico set the stage for his future work with psychedelics. Alongside his colleague Frank Barron, Leary continued to explore the potential of the human nervous system through the use of substances like psilocybin. They rented a villa in Cuernavaca, where they spent their days planning the framework for their research project. During one of their stays, an anthropologist from the University of Mexico, Gerhart Braun, visited and shared a small bag of psilocybin mushrooms he had obtained from a curandera. After some hesitation, Leary decided to try the mushrooms, marking the beginning of his exploration into hallucinogenic experiences. As the effects took hold, Leary observed that everything around him seemed to quiver and come alive, deepening his conviction that these substances held untapped potential for human consciousness.

Leary's journey into the world of psychedelics would soon become the cornerstone of his research at Harvard

Leary Returns to Harvard

Return to Harvard – Frank Barron - Video link

https://youtu.be/0GK9VzhhWBc

In September 1960 Leary arrived back at Harvard and moved into Newton Center with his two children.

"On the day I checked in for the fall semester I ran into George Litwin, considered one of the brightest graduate students in the department. During the preceding spring, when he had told me of some mescaline experiments he had performed on himself and others, I had voiced disapproval. At the time it sounded like chemical meddling.

I pulled him into my office and poured out the story of the mushroom session in Mexico. Litwin was delighted that my interest in altered states

107

had been awakened. He agreed to join the research project. In a few days several other graduate students came around to volunteer their services.

The following is from George Litwin

When he returned in the fall, he rushed up to me (George Litwin), and said we must immediately begin research on these mind-expanding chemicals, such as the psilocybe mushroom from Mexico. He selected me because I had done prior research with mescaline, and had spent a number of hours with him discussing the details of the mescaline sessions, and the possibilities for using this class of chemicals to expand consciousness and awareness of both self and environment.

We sat down that very afternoon and wrote a letter to Sandoz Pharmaceuticals, the company that first extracted the psilocybin from the mushroom, and then synthesized it in the laboratory. We expected a package of forms to fill out. Instead Sandoz sent us a large bottle of psilocybin pills and a brief note saying we should report back to them on any results we found.

1960

Sandoz Pharmaceutical began producing psilocybin pills, called Indocybin. Each pill contained 2 mg of psilocybin.

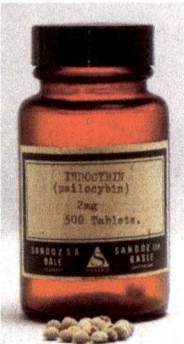

"(The) purpose of the research was to "determine the conditions under which psilocybin can be used to broaden and deepen human experience; to determine which persons are benefited by the drug, and in which direction; and to determine methods of making the beneficial effects durable and recoverable without subsequent exposure to the chemical."

Timothy Leary Letter to David McClelland - November 1960,

The psilocybin arrived shortly in pill form from the Sandoz branch in Hanover, New Jersey. The dosages varied and were administered according to mutual agreement. Using a detailed questionnaire, a record was kept of the impressions and experiences of each subject.

Just before Thanksgiving a cardboard box with four small brown bottles arrived. Printed on the label was the exciting admonition: not to be SOLD: for RESEARCH investigation. Under the plastic stopper there was a wad of cotton in the neck of the bottle. I shook out a few of the pills, which glistened like pink pearls in my hand. We stared at them, thinking solemn thoughts. The lives of all of us would be transformed by these tabs.

The Team - Graduate Students

At 5 Divinity Avenue, inside a small Harvard building, it felt like witnessing a science fiction story unfold in real time. The premise was simple: respected scientists set out to study the effects of indigenous psychedelic substances. But upon their return, they spoke in near-reverent tones of love and ecstatic revelation, insisting that no one could truly grasp reality until they had crossed the threshold—into another realm, beyond the Door. The transformation was reminiscent of *Invasion of the Body Snatchers*, the cult classic of the 1950s. Each day, more students and junior faculty squeezed into Leary's cramped office, their eyes alight, their voices hushed but urgent, discussing the death of conventional thought and the awakening of the mind's untapped potential.

And yet, it had all started in the most unassuming way—just another summer research project. Faculty often used the break to recharge, returning with fresh ideas and ambitious experiments. At first, Leary's enthusiasm seemed no different. Everyone knew he was studying Mexican mushrooms, and rumors of his lofty claims drifted from his tiny office. Comparisons to Galileo's telescope and even the discovery of fire weren't uncommon. Still, the project sounded more anthropological than psychological, and few took notice.

Leary's attempts to rally interest were met with indifference. When he invited senior faculty to experience psilocybin firsthand, only the aging Henry Murray took him up on the offer. Even after Murray described an astonishing vision—standing before an ancient Egyptian pyramid, watching a golden fountain erupt into the sky—no one seemed moved. That's when it hit Leary: his colleagues, trained psychologists, had no curiosity about their own unconscious minds. He had spent years criticizing the rigid, conformity-driven psychology of the 1950s, and now, confronted with its limitations, he saw just how deeply entrenched they were.

As Niels Bohr famously remarked, "A new scientific truth does not triumph by convincing its opponents, but rather because its opponents eventually die, and a new generation grows up familiar with it." Leary found his allies among the younger crowd—doctoral candidates like George Litwin, who had already experimented with mescaline, and Gunther Weil, a Fulbright scholar who joined the project immediately. Litwin suggested *The Doors of Perception* and *Heaven and Hell* by Aldous Huxley as foundational reading.

Leary, ever the charismatic persuader, soon amassed a devoted group of graduate students. This alarmed senior faculty, who viewed graduate students as a shared resource rather than Leary's personal recruits. Frank Barron, more mindful of academic politics, advised Leary to keep the project small to avoid resentment. But Leary was undeterred—he saw psychedelics as the key to the future and refused to turn away those eager to help forge it.

The core team included Ralph Metzner, Gunther Weil, Michael Kahn, George Litwin, and Ralph Schwitzgebel. Others, such as Pearl Chan, Michael Hollingshead, Walter Pahnke, Al Alschuler, Paul Lee, Rolf von Eckartberg, Huston Smith, James Ciarlo, Jonathan Shay, and Frank Ferguson, also joined the fold. With Richard Alpert's help, Leary assembled an extraordinary team, each member contributing their own strengths to what felt like a mission destined to redefine psychological research. Over time, they became more than colleagues—they were a tightly knit community, with Leary and Alpert as their guiding figures. Gunther Weil jokingly referred to them as "psychedelic mom and dad," with Alpert in the nurturing maternal role and Leary as the exuberant, authoritative father figure.

Alpert later embraced this dynamic, recalling, "I was the wife. I made the meals. I looked after the group. I was ready to dedicate my life to Timothy because I saw in him a true visionary—someone who could stand apart from the system and really see." He envisioned himself as the loyal second-in-command, standing just behind the captain as they navigated uncharted waters.

Each student found a unique role within what Litwin later dubbed "the boys' club." Litwin, raised on the rough streets of Detroit, brought organizational skills that the free-spirited academics lacked. "They were wild rebels," he later reflected. "Timothy was always stirring things up, and Dick often played the bridge to the outside world, trying to keep things from going completely off the rails."

Gunther Weil, steeped in jazz and the rhythms of Charlie Parker, was the group's cultural bridge to the Beat movement, while Ralph Metzner provided intellectual grounding, his sharp analytical mind and encyclopedic knowledge keeping the team's work rigorous. Weil described Metzner as "the German Oxford academic" whose insight and precision shaped much of their research.

Together, they formed a dynamic force, bound by an experience that defied explanation to outsiders. What began as an academic pursuit had become something far greater—an unprecedented journey into the mind's hidden dimensions, pushing beyond the limits of Harvard and into the undiscovered depths of human consciousness.

George Litwin writes about Leary 60 years Later

George Litwin, c. 1961

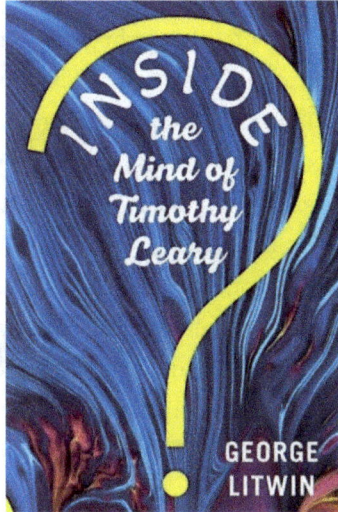

About the Author

George H. Litwin is a psychologist with a PhD in Social Psychology, with concentration in Personality Research, from Harvard University. He first met Timothy Leary at Harvard and continued to work with him throughout the many phases of Leary's career.

George Litwin had the extraordinary good fortune to be present at all of the psychedelic sessions described in this book. He was there when well-known pioneers like Aldous Huxley and others explored LSD and psilocybin. These revelations have never before been shared. This book offers a unique window into the history of psychedelics and psychology. Together with Timothy Leary, Richard Alpert/Baba Ram Dass, and Ralph Metzner, George Litwin is considered one of the founders of the psychedelic movement.

Gunther Weil

Tim was my assigned faculty advisor when I began my graduate studies at Harvard in the fall of 1960. That summer I had just returned from a year in Europe where I had been studying linguistic philosophy and psychology on a Fulbright Fellowship and began working as a graduate assistant with Harry Murray on some Thematic Apperception Test research. I remember being greeted enthusiastically by Tim as I entered his tiny office at the Center for Personality Research to discuss my graduate studies program. He displayed a keen interest in my philosophical leanings, particularly my growing interest in metaphysics and then shared with me some of the insights that he had received in Cuernavaca, Mexico from his psilocybin mushroom experience, and how this had led to his desire to initiate a research program to integrate this deep transactional understanding of altered consciousness into clinical psychology and therapy. Although I did not really understand what he was talking about, my experiences with marijuana in the late I 950's bebop jazz scene prompted my curiosity.Tim invited me to join the research team and I immediately accepted.Two weeks later Karen and I were married and I also had my first psilocybin session at Tim's home in Newton, Massachusetts. One of the most striking memories of this experience was to hear Tim quoting verbatim passages from James Joyce's Finnegan's Wake. He was totally inside the character and completely conversant with the cadence and meter and meaning. I was astounded and this certainly reinforced my interest in further exploration. – Gunther Weil

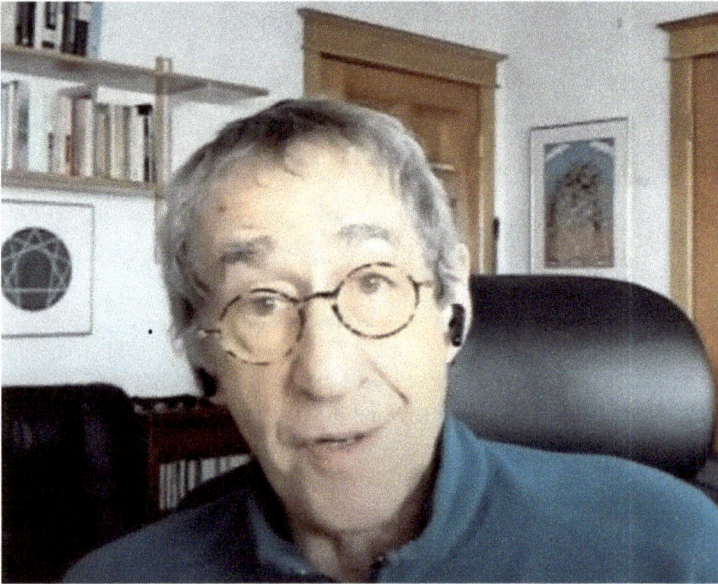

Watch Ed Reither with Gunther Weil - 2023

https://www.youtube.com/watch?v=Ef35IX5TGdk&t=1592s

Frank Barron

https://www.youtube.com/watch?v=e5av6wHug-0

After the experience, Leary in his excitement, drove to McClelland's place nearby in the hopes he would understand his new awakening. McCelland didn't but he did care for Leary and believed in his existential-transactional theories of behavior change and wanted very much to work together to humanize psychology.

Leary sketched a proposal for systematic drug experiments at Harvard. As his faculty sponsor, he was understandably alarmed at the administrative and political problems this kind of research could foresee down the line.

During the meeting with McClelland Leary realized that it was practically impossible to convey the experience of altered states to someone who hadn't been there. (I remembered my negative reaction to Barron when he tried to relate his mushroom experiences to me.) Even the most supporting friend looked at you with skepticism. So you saw bizarre things? You made yourself crazy for six hours? So? What does this have to do with practical problems of normal life?

I tried to explain to McClelland. The activity of every sense organ was intensified. Colors and shapes were fresh and clear. I became every musical instrument. Everything was alive. Even inanimate objects sent signals, took on meaning.

Later when Barron arrived Leary told him about McClelland's resistance, and Barron warned Leary about the compulsive tendency to run around explaining to everyone about the experience he had.

Later, Leary would find that the world was divided into those who had had the experience and those who had not and that is where the difficulties lay.

It became self-evident that emotional connections developed between those who had mind-expanding experience and those that hadn't. The sharing of the secret about the potential of the brain later became a significant and widespread social phenomenon.

Frank and I agreed to start a research project at Harvard to pursue this further. Frank would concentrate on the creativity aspect, while I would work on using the drugs to accelerate behavior change.

"Harvard seemed to be the ideal university for this even psychologist and philosopher William James, a previous lecturer at this elite university and founder of the profession of psychology in the United States, was acquainted with psychedelic experiences."

Flashbacks, Timothy Leary

Looking for Guidance

Aldous Huxley

Aldous Huxley lecturing at M.I.T. 1960

In the fall semester 1960 Aldous Huxley was the Carnegie Visiting Professor of Humanities at the Massachusetts Institute of Technology (M.I.T). He presented a series of lectures concerning history, language, and art under the title **"What a Piece of Work is a Man."**

Aldous Huxley was staying in a new M.l.T. apartment overlooking the Charles River. He answered the bell - tall, pale, frail - joined me, and we drove to the Harvard Faculty Club

119

On November 8, 1960, Humphry Osmond brought Huxley and Leary together at a luncheon in Boston. After their meeting Huxley offered to consult with them and suggested they also invite Huston Smith, professor of comparative religion at the Massachusetts Institute of Technology (MIT) in Boston to join the project.

We talked about how to study and use the consciousness-expanding drugs and we clicked along agreeably on the do's and not-to-do's. We would avoid the behaviorist approach to others awareness. Avoid labeling or depersonalizing the subject. We should not impose our own jargon or our own experimental games on others. We were not out to discover new laws, which is to say, to discover the redundant implications of our own premises. We were not to be limited by the pathological point of view. We were not to interpret ecstacy as mania, or calm serenity as catatonia; we were not to diagnose Buddha as a detached schizoid; nor Christ as an exhibitionistic masochist; nor the mystic experience as a symptom; nor the visionary state as a model psychosis. Aldous Huxley, chuckling away with compassionate humour at human folly.

And with such erudition! Moving back and forth in history, quoting the mystics. Wordsworth. Plotinus. The Areopagite. William James. Ranging from the esoteric past, back to the biochemical present: Humphrey Osmond curing alcoholics in Saskatchewan with LSD; Keith Ditman's plans to clean out Skid Row in Los Angeles with LSD; Roger Heim taking his bag of Mexican mushrooms to the Parisian chemists who couldn't isolate the active ingredient, and then going to Albert Hofmann the great Swiss, who did it and called it psilocybin. They had sent the pills back to the curandera in Oaxaca state and she tried them and had divinatory visions and was happy that her practice could now be a year-round and not restrained to three raining mushroom months.

Aldous Huxley was shrewdly aware of the political complications and the expected opposition from the Murugans, the name he gave to power people in his novel, 'Island'

What's the name?... Answer, practically everything... Murugan calls it dope and feels about it all the disapproval that, by conditioned reflex, the dirty word evokes. We on the contrary, give the stuff good names - the moksha - medicine, the reality- revealer, the truth-and-beauty pill. And we know, by direct experience, that the good names are deserved. Whereas our young friend here has no first-hand knowledge of the stuff and can't be persuaded even to give it a try. For him, it's dope and dope is something that, by definition, no decent person ever indulges in.

Aldous Huxley advised and counselled and joked and told stories and we listend and our research project was shaped accordingly. Huxley offered to sit in on our planning meetings and was ready to take mushrooms with us when the research was under way.

From these meetings grew the design for a naturalistic pilot study, in which the subjects would be treated like astronauts - carefully prepared, briefed with all available facts, and then expected to run their own spacecraft, make their own observations, and report back to ground control Our subjects were not passive patients but hero-explorers.

During the weeks of October and November 1960 there were many meetings to plan the research. Aldous Huxley would come and listen and then close his eyes and detach himself from the scene and go into his controlled meditation trance, which was unnerving to some of the Harvard people who equate consciousness with talk, and then he would open his eyes and make a diamond-pure

To guide us in these experimental rituals Aldous Huxley brought over a description by Theophile Gautier of the techniques used by Baudelaire and the *Hashish Club of Paris* (1844-1849) one hundred years earlier:

It is understood, then, if one wishes to enjoy to the full the magic hashish, it is necessary to prepare in advance and furnish in some way the *motif* to its extravagant variations and disorderly fantasies. It is important to be in a tranquil frame of mind and body, to have on this day neither anxiety, duty, nor fixed time, and to find oneself in such an apartment as Baudelaire and Edgar Poe loved, a room furnished with poetical comfort, bizarre luxury, and mysterious elegance; a private and hidden retreat....

In such circumstances, it is probable, and even almost certain, that the naturally agreeable sensations turn into ravishing blessings, ecstasies, ineffable pleasure, much superior to the coarse joys promised to the faithful in the paradise of Mahomet....Baudelaire - His Life and Times

First Session in Cambridge - Fall 1960

THE FIRST PSYCHEDELIC SESSION IN CAMBRIDGE

The Timothy Leary Project - Jennifer Ulrich

The first psilocybin psychedelic session in Cambridge during the Leary era.

During the summer of 1960, Tim had stayed in Mexico with a colleague, Frank Barron, and they decided to hire a curandera who was experienced in taking psilocybe mushrooms and guiding sessions. She was older, and from the region north of Oaxaca in the mountains. Timothy had a very positive experience with the psilocybe mushrooms.

When he returned in the fall, he rushed up to me (George Litwin), and said we must immediately begin research on these mind-expanding chemicals, such as the psilocybe mushroom from Mexico. He selected me because I had done prior research with mescaline, and had spent a number of hours with him discussing the details of the mescaline sessions, and the

122

possibilities for using this class of chemicals to expand consciousness and awareness of both self and environment.

We sat down that very afternoon and wrote a letter to Sandoz Pharmaceuticals, the company that first extracted the psilocybin from the mushroom, and then synthesized it in the laboratory. We expected a package of forms to fill out. Instead Sandoz sent us a large bottle of psilocybin pills and a brief note saying we should report back to them on any results we found. Timothy took the pills for safe-keeping. Several weeks later, he called me on a Sunday afternoon and said, "Aldous Huxley is visiting and he wants to try psilocybin. I think we will do the session this afternoon. Do you want to join us?"

They did have the session in the afternoon and after they got together in the kitchen of Leay's house. Timothy talked about his experience and compared it with his experience with the mushroom in Mexico. Aldous compared the psilocybin experience with other psychedelic experiences he had had. He said he thought the psilocybin was much gentler and less disturbing than drugs such as LSD. In that light, he thought it might have a positive social value.

The team afterward decided that with the lower dosages of psilocybin (four to eight milligrams) there would be perhaps better a better research dosage and also quite comfortable to return from the session and be able to share the experience better for the research project.

The Experiments Begin

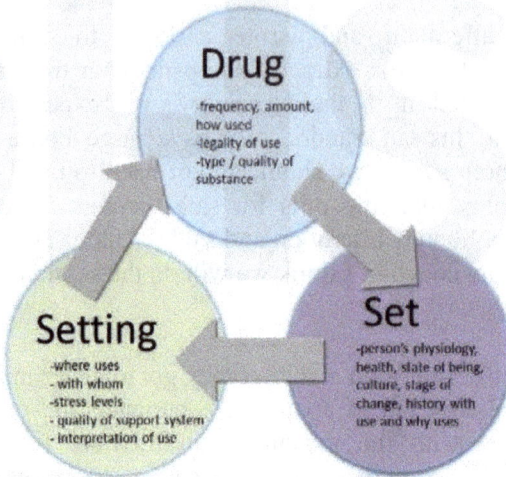

Their next few weeks were devoted to experimental sessions with the drug. It was a naive romantic time. We were excited by the notion that we humans could fly, cut loose the synaptic cords that held us to low levels of mentation, soar into uncharted realms of the brain. It was Wright Brothers season as each novice took off, sometimes wobbly and then sailing out beyond normal consciousness. Hey Wilbur, watch that tree! Orville, how are you doing? One by one we flight trainees would fly out beyond our radars, get lost within, and then swoop back for landings with wondrous tales.

We were on our own. Western psychological literature had almost no guides, no maps, no texts that even recognized the existence of altered states. We had no rituals, traditions, or comforting routines to fall back on. In line with our existential-transactional theories we avoided the sterility of the laboratory and the sick-man atmosphere of the hospital. We conducted the experiments in faculty homes, in front of comforting fireplaces, with candles instead of electric lights, and evocative music.

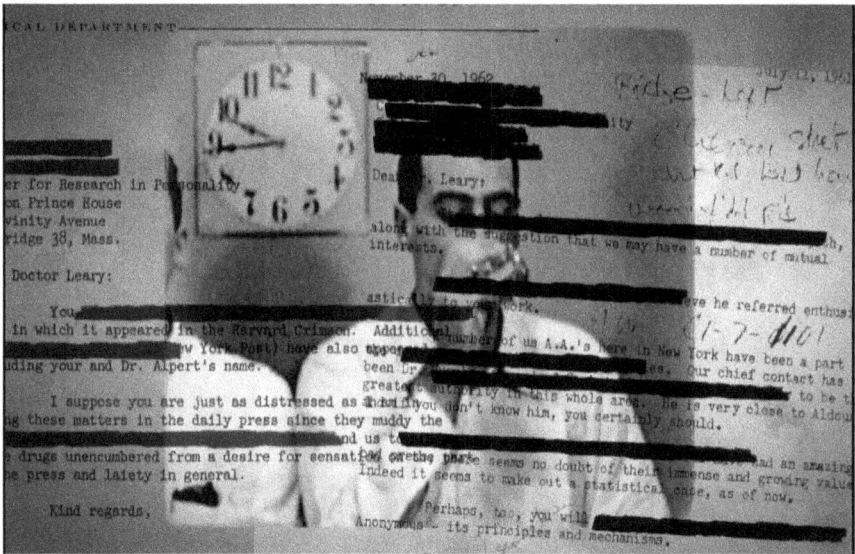

The project in concert with David McLelland was designed to study the effects of psilocybin on Harvard graduate students and others who qualified and were interested. Over almost three years of its operation, it was said to have administered (documented) close to 400 trials to willing and informed participants.

The seeds of political troubles with other faculty started during the initial meetings of the group when they decided to make the research existential-transactional, meaning the experiments would not follow the medical model of giving drugs to others and then observing only external results. Quite the opposite. The academic scientists would teach themselves how

125

to use drugs and how to run sessions. They were using a new kind of microscope, one which made visible an extraordinary range of new perceptions. Their first task was to develop experimental manuals on how to focus the new tools. These young scientists, newly trained, could then use the drugs on themselves and others to study how it affected them and, therefore, had some sense of its capacities.

First, they had to obtain the drugs. George Litwin said that Sandoz Laboratories, the Swiss firm that discovered LSD, had synthesized the active ingredient of the mushrooms and that their branch office in New Jersey.

Richard Alpert working with Ralph Metzner, 1960

THE EXPERIENTIAL TYPEWRITER

TIMOTHY LEARY

IN EARLIER PAPERS, (1, 2, 3), we have stressed the importance of the astonishing statistics about the nervous system and the potentialities of consciousness. For us these neurological numbers take on the meaning of mantras.

THE HUMAN BRAIN
RECEIVES
ONE THOUSAND MILLION SIGNALS
A
SECOND

OR

WE POSSESS
BETWEEN
TEN AND THIRTEEN
BILLION
BRAIN CELLS

OR

EACH BRAIN CELL
IS CONNECTED
(ON THE AVERAGE)
WITH TWENTY-FIVE THOUSAND
OTHER CELLS

During an ecstatic experience triggered by psychedelic foods and drugs we are tuned in to some of this astonishing neural activity. Billions of signals are being registered, decoded a minute. Thousands of energy languages are operating each minute. Each level of energy defines a level of consciousness.

There were 38 subjects the majority were postgraduate students and colleagues at the university, along with good friends. Leary and Alpert procured the psilocybin in pill form from the Sandoz branch in Hanover, New Jersey. The dosages varied and were administered according to mutual agreement. Using a detailed questionnaire, a record was kept of the impressions and experiences of each subject. Three-quarters of them

127

described very pleasant experiences and nearly as many a noticeable expansion of consciousness

One dominant result that came from the first experiments were Leary and Alpert considered psilocybin had the ability to enhance mental capabilities and creativity and recommended it as instant psychoanalysis for use in psychotherapy. To avoid the term drug, they called psilocybin a consciousness-expanding substance.

Susan Homer, Richard, Tim and Peggy, Newton Center, 1963

Test Subjects

Subjects

During the course of this first naturalistic study we administered psilocybin to 175 subjects, of which 12% were men and 48 were women. The median age was 29.5 years,, with 70% of the subjects falling in the range 22 to 35 years.

All subjects were volunteers and unpaid. The selection factor constitutes an important limitation. During the past 18 months we have been engaged in lecturing and talking to many people about psilocybin. We estimate that of those who hear about our work, one third are immediately and intensely interested, one third neutral and one third have strong reservations about participating in such a project. The subjects of this study do not sample this wide a range of initial reactions. Most of our subjects naturally come from the first group.

Occupationally, the subjects included graduate graduate students, professional writers and artists, academic psychologists, musicians, housewives, and inmates in a correctional institution.

Dosage

Dosage

Most previous research with psilocybin used dosages around 5-10 mg. In our work we found it useful to allow a much wider range of dosage. We established a reasonable and safe limit and allowed subjects to determine their own dosage under this limit. As we gained experience we raised this limit somewhat. Our more or less stable position has been that 0.5 mg. per kg. of body weight is a reasonable limit to set for a 6-8 hour period.

With respect to dosage, 20 to 30 milligrams seems to provide an optimal initial experience in a group setting. Higher dosages, around 50 milligrams, were taken by subjects experienced in drug use who wanted to have a "deep" experience.

After six weeks we had run sessions for fifteen staff members. We learned a lot about dosage and the importance of setting—the tone of the environment, which included the people attending a session. We soon discovered that strong bonds developed among those who shared a session. They seemed to need to see each other, be close to each other for the week after the experience. For this reason we decided that each explorer should be allowed to invite family members and close friends to participate.

Our excitement naturally provoked concern among other faculty members. Almost all of the graduate students at the Center signed up for brain-drug training, which caused a predictable jealousy. According to ancient custom every student was apprenticed to assist the research of a senior faculty member. The swarming of students to the drug project became a hot in-house political issue. Frank Barron and I talked to our faculty colleagues and offered to set up sessions for them, but most declined the experience. They had no paradigms by which to understand this new phenomenon, so they weren't interested. They simply wanted their allotment of graduate students back.

Inevitably we mushroom researchers began to hang out together, enjoying the deep attachments and enthusiasms that pioneers always share, meanwhile drifting away from former friends. The trip was so powerful, so different, so shattering to one's illusion of a single reality that the people who had experienced it inevitably formed an in-group. The differences between those who wanted to explore new brain terrain and those who reflexively avoided the challenge foreshadowed the bitter cultural conflict that raged everywhere in the decade to come.

The question that haunted our work in those early days was: how could we introduce these methods for mind expansion to society? - Flashbacks, p. 43

The university administration noted the successful experiments and amazing results but was unable to dismiss concerns about the utility of the project. However, the enthusiastic reports awakened curiosity among the students and their friends. Some experienced a marvelous psychedelic experience at Leary's house or elsewhere in private quarters without being officially part of a study.

Increasingly, a noticeable boundary formed between those who had had a psilocybin experience and those who did not belong to the inner circle of the initiated. - Mystic Chemist, pp.139

Introduction to the Program Statement and Scholarly Journal Publication

In the early 1960s, Harvard University's Center for Research in Personality, under the leadership of Dr. Timothy Leary and Dr. Richard Alpert, launched an ambitious study on psilocybin, the psychoactive compound found in psychedelic mushrooms. Their research, both innovative and controversial, became a defining moment in the scientific investigation of altered states of consciousness. This era of experimentation laid the groundwork for modern psychedelic studies. The two documents presented here—a Program Statement from the Harvard research team and

131

a scholarly journal article detailing their findings—offer firsthand insight into their goals, methods, and initial discoveries.

The *Program Statement* outlines the team's objectives and theoretical perspective. It highlights psilocybin's potential to facilitate deep personal insights, alter cognitive patterns, and strengthen interpersonal connections. Importantly, the researchers identified that the drug's effectiveness was not solely chemical but also dependent on environmental factors—what they termed "set and setting." This principle later became a cornerstone of psychedelic research. The statement emphasizes their goal of conducting studies in a structured, supportive, and human-centered environment, as opposed to the detached clinical settings traditionally used in psychiatric experiments.

The *Scholarly Journal Publication, Reactions to Psilocybin Administered in a Supportive Environment*, expands on these ideas with empirical data and theoretical discussion. Written by Leary, George H. Litwin, and Ralph Metzner, the article positions their findings within the broader scientific discourse on consciousness. It challenges the classification of psychedelics as merely 'psychotomimetic'—substances that induce states similar to psychosis—arguing instead for their potential to produce mystical or religious experiences. The study also examines the biochemical aspects of psilocybin, emphasizing its non-addictive properties and its ability to induce perceptual changes beyond conventional psychological categories.

These two documents illustrate not only the excitement and intellectual curiosity that fueled Leary and Alpert's research but also the tensions their work created within Harvard. As interest in psychedelics grew, students flocked to the research program, leading to concerns among faculty members. Some saw the project as an unwelcome disruption, sparking an internal political struggle. This divide—between those open to exploring new frontiers of consciousness and those resistant to such shifts—anticipated the broader cultural conflicts that defined the 1960s.

Ultimately, the Harvard psychedelic research program ended in controversy, but its legacy continues to shape contemporary discussions on consciousness, mental health, and the therapeutic applications of psychedelics. By revisiting these primary documents, readers gain a direct perspective on the original vision that inspired this movement, as well as the challenges faced in bringing these ideas to the mainstream.

PROGRAM STATEMENT

Harvard University Center for Research and Personality, A Program of Research with Consciousness Altering Substances Introduction.

We at Harvard, under the instigation and direction of Dr. Timothy Leary, have been exploring in some depth the uses of consciousness-altering substances. In our work, we have used several different substances, LSD, mescaline, and psilocybin. We continue to be interested in the potential of all of these. In the course of these investigations, however, we have concentrated on the use of psilocybin because of certain advantages. Specifically, these advantages are,

(1) the duration of the major effect of the drug is short, about five hours.

(2) There are minimal somatic side effects, and

(3), there are few cultural preconceptions regarding its effect.

From our experiences to date, in addition to reports from other investigators, we have come to believe that psilocybin has the potential to facilitate for an individual the experience of major insights and problem solutions of an intellectual, emotional nature. The realm of these insights or problem solutions is in any area which is meaningful to that individual, be it social or personal, intellectual, religious, philosophical, etc.

It is our conviction that these insights, enlightenment, or solutions provide a firm educational foundation for (a) change in the social or intellectual behavior of the individual, (b) the development of new models regarding the nature of man, along with suitable research designs to test such models, (c) the development of more subtle methods of communication between individuals and, (d) the conceptualization and formulation of modified social systems.

To all of us who have participated in this research, it is evident that bringing about such effects involves far more than the psilocybin itself. Any number of rituals and reactions can be related to the taking of a consciousness, expanding substance. In order for the educational value of the experience to be fully realized, it is necessary to provide a set for the individual and a warm, supportive, and genuinely human setting for the experience, all of which are maximally conducive to the gaining of insight or enlightenment and to change.

The data on which we are basing our efforts is mainly our own subjective experiences, as well as reports of reactions of others who have participated in our sessions. Certain of these reactions, which seem most significant, are:

(1) An experience of disassociation or detachment that is the feeling of oneself as separate from the roles, rules, rituals, values, methods of communication, and goals with which one is involved in daily life.

(2) The feeling that one is free to change, relearn, grow, and pursue new goals.

(3) The feeling of profound receptivity and the ability to engage the surrounding world of man and nature. Particularly powerful are the feelings of closeness, empathy, and openness with others with whom one has shared a psilocybin session. Individuals often report no longer feeling isolated or alienated, but rather feeling themselves to be part of a larger

identity. ("Ask not for whom The bell tolls...") From this emerges a fundamental concern, not in the sense of one being for another, but in the sense of one, part of an identity for other, another part of itself.

4) The close contact referred to in the above has certain elements that suggest increased sensitivity to others, moods, thoughts and feelings, and greatly facilitated communication with them through both verbal and non-verbal means.

It is from these basic subjective reactions that many of our ideas regarding the potential of these experiences, as well as the methods of researching them, have been derived.

A large body of medical and psychiatric opinion regards, psilocybin and similar substances as "psychotomemetic" i.e. as producing temporary "model psychosis." Certainly there are similarities, e.g. the increased importance of primary process thought mechanisms, but there are other also profound differences, e.g, absence of fear, maintenance of a voluntary control and rational functioning. Further, it should not be forgotten that most of the work on the "model psychosis" has been carried out in mental hospitals, usually in cold clinical, observe and patient situations, observer and patient situations, such situations are not conducive to a good or even coherent experience, but rather naturally foster fear, suspicion, and helplessness.

Our goal, however, is to arrange optimally therapeutic and educational experience in warm, supportive environments. Therefore, our present plans do not include a direct comparison to the psycho two memetic and conscious expanding experiences within the usual experiential framework.

Scholarly Journal Publication

The Relation of Expectation and Mood to Psilocybin Reactions: A Questionaire Study, Ralph Metzner, George Litwin & Gunther Weil. The Psychedelic Review, 1965, Vol 5, pp 3-39.

Reprinted from THE JOURNAL OF NERVOUS AND MENTAL DISEASE
Vol. 137, No. 6   December, 1963
Copyright © 1963 by The Williams & Wilkins Co.
Printed in U.S.A.

Center for Research in Personality, Harvard University, Cambridge. Massachusetts.

The authors wish to express their gratitude to Dr. Carl Henze and Mr. Sidney Gimpel of Sandoz Laboratories, which supplied psilocybin, and to Richard Alpert, Gunther Weil, Sheila Sostek and Mrs. Pearl Chan for their cooperation and help.

This project was supported in part by grants from the Uris Brothers Foundation and from the Laboratory of Social Relations, Harvard University.

REACTIONS TO PSILOCYBIN ADMINISTERED IN A SUPPORTIVE ENVIRONMENT

TIMOTHY LEARY, Ph.D.,[1] GEORGE H. LITWIN, A.B.[1] AND RALPH METZNER, Ph.D.[1]

In recent decades Western civilization has discovered that the ingestion of certain plants can produce astonishing effects upon human consciousness. This information has been held for centuries by certain nonliterate tribes who have used the plants in religious and medical procedures. Interest in these substances has been stimulated by the achievement of chemists, most notably Dr. Albert Hofmann, of the Sandoz Laborato-

Both from our own observations and from a survey of the literature one may conclude: 1) that these substances are not "addictive" (2), i.e., although tolerance develops, no case of addiction has ever been reported; 2) they are neither sedatives nor tranquilizers—subjects often report heightened sensitivity to stimuli and excitability and there is no evidence that the drugs have anxiety-reducing effects; 3) they cannot be classed with

REACTIONS TO PSILOCYBIN ADMINISTERED INA SUPPORTIVE ENVIRONMENT

TIMOTHY LEARY, Ph.D., GEORGE H. LITWIN, A.B. and RALPH METZNER, Ph.D.

In recent decades Western civilization has discovered that the ingestion of certain plants can produce astonishing effects upon human consciousness. This information has been held for centuries by certain nonliterate tribes who have used the plants in religious and medical procedures.

Interest in these substances has been stimulated by the achievement of chemists, most notably Dr. Albert Hofmann, of the Sandoz Laboratories in Basel, Switzerland, who have succeeded in synthesizing the active agents in these plants.

137

Among these the best known are the:

(1) Peyote cactus, from which mescaline is derived,

2) The mushroom *psilocybe mexicana,* the South American vine *yage* or *caapi,* and

(3) The seed of *ololiuqui,* also from Mexico.

The substance used in a recent study is *psilocybin,* a synthetic of the Mexican "sacred mushroom" introduced to Americans by the mycologist R. Gordon Wasson. The active ingredient, psilocybin, was synthesized by Dr. Hofmann in 1959.

The physiological action of these drugs is not well understood, although some investigators have suggested that the common biochemical denominator may be the indole nucleus, which is found in most of these drugs and is also in serotonin. Elkes provided an excellent review of the relevant literature.

Both from our own observations and from a survey of the literature one may conclude:

(1) That these substances are not "addictive".

(2) Although tolerance develops, no case of addiction has ever been reported.

(3) They are neither sedatives nor tranquilizers. Subjects often report heightened sensitivity to stimuli and excitability and there is no evidence that the drugs have anxiety-reducing effects.

(4) They cannot be classed with energizers or stimulants, since although there is increased sensitivity there is usually a reduction in task-oriented

138

energy, and subjects often sit very quietly. Although some investigators have classified these drugs as "psychotomimetic" *(i.e.,* as inducing "model psychoses"), others have reported that "mystical" or "religious" experiences are produced.

It is clear from these disagreements that attempts at strict categorization of the effects of these materials are premature.

It is the present hypothesis that the attitude of the experimenter toward the subject matter is an important variable. It influences the expectation or set which he or she communicates to their subjects, and it determines what kind of setting they provide for the ingestion of the drug; these in turn have marked effects on the nature of the experience.

Most investigators would, however, agree to the statement that these drugs alter consciousness.

The purpose of the present research was to investigate some of the ways in which consciousness may be altered. The two major practical difficulties in carrying out such an inquiry are

(1) the role of set and suggestion, mentioned above, and

(2) the fact that both everyday and scientific language are extremely inadequate for describing altered states of consciousness.

Reaching Out - Meets with Richard Evans

HARVARD UNIVERSITY
DEPARTMENT OF SOCIAL RELATIONS

CENTER FOR RESEARCH IN PERSONALITY
MORTON PRINCE HOUSE

5 Divinity Avenue
Cambridge 38, Massachusetts

December 9, 1960

Mr. Robert Gordon Wasson
1 East End Avenue
New York, N.Y.

Dear Mr. Wasson:

Supper with you and your family remains a pleasant and inspiring memory. I continue to be impressed by what you have done in opening up important new fields to science—and even more impressed by the possibilities related to your central position in this field. In regard to the latter I have consulted with the Director of this Center and obtained his enthusiastic response to the proposal that you visit Harvard to lead a symposium on your work. I have also contacted Dr. Schultes, who also approved of this plan.

How does this tentative program sound to you?

1. Would you care to address the faculty and graduate students of the Social Relations Department (psychology, sociology, anthropology)? Announcements of your talk would be sent to other departments interested in your work, including botany, pharmacology, medical school.

2. Would you be willing to spend the rest of the day meeting with small groups of staff members who have technical interest in your work?

While we cannot hope to recompense you adequately for the experience and wisdom you would bring with you, we would be happy to cover your expenses and offer the token consultant compensation of one hundred dollars.

I would be honored if you would stay with me as my guest during your visit. However, if it would be more convenient I could arrange space for you at the Harvard Faculty Club.

During our evening together we spoke of a second matter which I consider of equal importance—the possibility of providing clerical help to organize a bibliography of publication about the mushroom. Research funds are available to me and I would view it as a happy duty to society to offer the temporary services of a person who could assist in this work.

I hope that you will find time from your busy schedule to join with us in these two vital programs.

Sincerely yours,

Timothy Leary

Schultes   TLds

140

April 10, 1961

Dr. Timothy Leary
Department of Social Relations
Center for Research in Personality
Harvard University
Morton Prince House
5 Divinity Avenue
Cambridge, Mass.

Dear Dr. Leary:

I am considerably disturbed by the arrangement of the bibliography. Perhaps we had better call the whole thing off. The Sandoz people agree that to mix the different aspects of the subject together is a step backward. My work in this field has always been, so far as I could make it, a fine product. I am unwilling to compromise now on a question of quality. To mix archeology with clinical work in hospitals makes no sense whatever.

I shall be back in the second half of May and we can discuss it then.

With kind regards,

As ever,

RG Wasson

The Authorities Get Wind

The Communication Problem

Thomas LaMont Overseer   Timothy Leary - Faculty   Nathan Pusey - President

Despite their best efforts to stick to the scientific method—based on logic and step-by-step thinking—it didn't take long for Leary and Alpert to realize that this approach wasn't going to cut it when it came to explaining psychedelic experiences. The human brain processes an incredible amount of information—about a billion signals every second, with trillions of connections firing between billions of brain cells. But language and logical thinking just can't keep up with what's happening during a psychedelic trip.

When someone takes psychedelics, the brain operates on many different levels of consciousness, far beyond our everyday awareness. The sheer speed and complexity of these brain activities make it impossible to fully describe in words. Even our best attempts to explain what's going on with language can only capture a tiny sliver of the experience. That's why, when

142

people try to explain what they felt, they often end up saying something simple, like "Wow!" because words just fall short.

What critics saw as a failure in Leary and Alpert's methods was actually their most groundbreaking discovery—and, in the end, part of what led to their downfall. They weren't failing at science. Instead, they were intentionally stepping outside the traditional scientific rules to explore consciousness in a way that had never been done before. They weren't rejecting work, politics, religion, or art. Rather, they were trying to push beyond those familiar roles by tapping into the brain's untapped potential and the mystical experiences it could offer.

In a response published in the *Harvard Review*, Leary and Alpert openly embraced the idea of a coming transformation in human consciousness. They believed that humanity was on the brink of unlocking the brain's full power, which could change the world as we know it. Instead of dismissing society's systems, they called for people to be open to new possibilities and to prepare for a major shift in how we understand ourselves and the world around us.

Moving off Campus

The Newton Center

In September of Leary's first year he along with his children the kids moved to what was soon to be called the 'Newton Center' at 64 Homer St, Newton. The soon to become center was located in a Boston suburb about five miles from Cambridge. The house was a three-story mansion on a hill with trees, lawns, a four-car garage, a garden gazebo, and 185 stone steps up to the front door. It was luxuriously furnished: wood paneling, thick rugs, plush sofas, Moroccan metalwork lamps. There was a wide staircase winding up from the entrance hall.

The house belonged to a professor taking his sabbatical in the Soviet Union.

144

The early experiments conducted by Timothy Leary and Richard Alpert at Harvard University's Social Research Center on Divinity Avenue initially held promise for advancing their research into the effects of psychedelics on human consciousness. However, the sterile and confined environment of the research center quickly became a hindrance to their work. The structured and academic setting was at odds with the expansive nature of the experiences they sought to explore, limiting both the range and depth of the outcomes.

Participants often found it difficult to engage fully with the experimental process in such a formalized and rigid atmosphere. The clinical setting was devoid of the natural or relaxed surroundings that Leary and Alpert believed were crucial for meaningful psychedelic experiences. As a result, the experiments produced data that, while useful, felt disconnected from the transformative potential they aimed to study.

Ultimately, the researchers realized that the environment of the Social Research Center was insufficient for the kind of personal and spiritual revelations they hoped to facilitate. The rigid boundaries of the university lab were not conducive to the holistic, open-ended experiences they were exploring, prompting them to move off campus. By seeking less restrictive and more natural environments, they hoped to create settings more aligned with the profound mental and spiritual states that their experiments sought to unlock.

Newton Center studies, Frank Ferguson (middle) and Barbara Dunlap (right)

The first psilocybin psychedelic session in Newton.

The Beats Enter

On November 26, Timothy Leary administered psilocybin to poet Allen Ginsberg and his partner, Peter Orlovsky. Ginsberg was no stranger to psychedelics, having previously experimented with peyote, mescaline, and LSD—his first experience with the latter occurring at Stanford University's hospital, the same place where novelist Ken Kesey was later introduced to the drug.

Ginsberg had come to Boston to speak at a meeting of the Group for the Advancement of Psychiatry, where he read from his poems *Laughing Gas*, *Mescaline*, and *Lysergic Acid*, which would soon be published in *Kaddish and Other Poems*. The reception was anything but warm. Younger psychiatrists dismissed him as clinically insane, while the older, Freudian-trained analysts interpreted his experiences as a complete ego disintegration, followed by a reintegration of the self in a slightly altered form. Only Humphry Osmond seemed to grasp what Ginsberg was trying to convey. Recognizing a shared understanding, Osmond and a colleague suggested that Ginsberg might benefit from meeting a Harvard psychologist conducting psychedelic research with funding from Sandoz Laboratories.

Back in New York City, intrigued by the prospect, Ginsberg wrote to the psychologist, expressing his eagerness to participate in the study. Within a week, Timothy Leary arrived at Ginsberg's East Village apartment. The poet was surprised and amused that a Harvard professor had come all the way to see him but found Leary somewhat naïve. It was clear to Ginsberg that Leary was unaware that nearly every poet he knew in San Francisco had already experimented with peyote, mescaline, and marijuana. Wasting no time, Ginsberg introduced Leary to cannabis and engaged him in a deep, scholarly conversation. The two immediately formed a strong connection. "I was surprised that he was such a jivey, friendly, amiable, open guy," Ginsberg later recalled. "And I saw right away that he saw me as a wise

Jewish patriarch with a family rather than a creepy beatnik. So I decided to go to Boston and experiment with him."

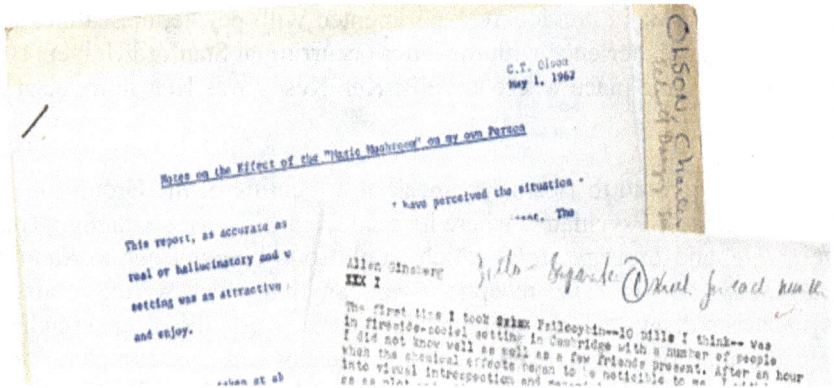

William Burroughs

'To reach the Western Lands is to achieve freedom from fear. Do you free yourself from fear by cowering in your physical body for eternity? Your body is a boat to lay aside when you reach the far shore, or sell it if you can find a fool... it's full of holes... it's full of holes.'

Burroughs WS (1987) The Western Lands. New York, Viking Penguin.

"In 1950 William Burrroughs' read an article in a popular science magazine at Grand Central Station that claimed that the medicine men of the Amazon and the Andean foothills used a decoction to foresee the future and communicate with the spirits of their ancestors. The story captured his interest and through further research in the New York Public Library he learned that Richard Spruce had identified the active ingredient in the shaman's potion in 1851 as a fast growing liana with a thick double helical stem that belonged to the tropical family of flowering plants known as the Malpighiaciae. Despite his lack of experience in botanical fieldwork, Burroughs embarked on his first serious attempt 'to dig yagé' in 1953.

On his arrival in the Colombian capital Burroughs took a tram to the Instituto de Ciencias Naturales of the Universidad Nacional de Colombia where he had the good fortune to bump into Doctor Richard Evans Schultes. Schultes was an ethnobotanist who had graduated from Harvard University a year after Burroughs.

Schultes was officially employed by the US Department of Agriculture to survey rubber production in the Amazon but as a result of his close collaboration with plant chemists in Boston he had succeeded in revealing the medicinal secrets of at least two hundred indigenous plants. Schultes pulled out a dry, wrinkled piece of caapi stem and told Burroughs that under its influence he had experienced hazy blue and grey colours. Schultes recommended that if Burroughs wanted to have an authentic experience, he should leave Bogotá and travel to Puerto Asis"

Timothy Leary, A Biography, Robert Greenfield, Chapter 12

HARVARD UNIVERSITY

DEPARTMENT OF SOCIAL RELATIONS

CENTER FOR RESEARCH IN PERSONALITY   5 DIVINITY AVENUE
MORTON PRINCE HOUSE   CAMBRIDGE 38, MASSACHUSETTS

December 6, 1960

Olympia Press
Paris
France

Gentlemen:

Would you please send me a copy of Naked Lunch
by William Burroughs. This book is needed in connection
with research I am doing on drugs and their effect
on creativity.

I am making arrangements with American customs
to see that this book can be admitted to the United
States.

Sincerely yours,

Timothy Leary

TL:ds

Letter to publisher, Maurice Girodias, Olympia Press

Charles Olson

December (and February 1961): Olson ingests synthetic psilocybin with Timothy Leary (recounted in a taped 1963 discussion, transcribed and published as "Under the Mushroom: the Gratwick Highlands Tape" in OLSON #3; reprinted in Muthologos; streaming audio at PennSound).

Jack Kerouac

After taking the mushrooms, Kerouac at least responded to Leary enough to write him a poem postcard and a "stupid drunken letter", detailing the experience he'd more or less refused to share at the time.

The letter is a little more of what Leary had wanted. It details the mental and physical impact of the drug on Kerouac:

Mainly I felt like a floating Kahn on a magic carpet with my interesting lieutenants and gods... some ancient feeling about old geheuls in the grass, and temples, exactly also like the sensation I got drunk on pulque floating in the Xochimilco gardens on barges laden with flowers and singers... some old Golden Age dream of man, very nice. But that is the element of hallucination in this acid called mushrooms (Amanita?) The bad physical side-effects involved (for me) stiffening of elbow and knee joints, a swelling of the eyelid, shortness of breath or rather anxiety about breathing itself. No heart palpitations like in mescaline, however… Yet there were no evil side effects.

In the letter, Kerouac also claims to have talked to his mother for three days, realizing he loved her more than he thought. He also claims to have awoken one morning convinced that the neighbours thought him "Master of Trust in Heaven." The world, he felt, was trustful and everyone around him was innocent.

He continued,

In sum, also, there is temporary addiction but no withdrawl symptoms whatever. The faculty of remembering names and what one has learned, is heightened so fantastically that we could develop the greatest scholars and scientists in the world with this stuff… There's no harm in Sacred Mushrooms if taken in moderation as a rule and much good will come of it.

This letter, however, was not shared as Leary wished. When Leary requested that it be published as evidence of the trip, Kerouac refused. In his journey he wrote negatively of the experience: "The psychic clairvoyance lasted till early this morning – I've been sleeping it off (too much to live with, in fact too much for Samahdi peace)." Not long after that, he began comparing the hallucinogenic experience to communist brainwashing. Moreover, Kerouac later made the claim that psilocybin had caused irreparable damage to his mind. "I haven't been right since," he dubiously claimed.

Timothy Leary, A Biography, Robert Greenfield, Chapter 12

Allen Ginsberg

On November 15, Tim Leary responded to a note from David McClelland, asking him to "put on record the design of our mushroom research." In a three-page letter, Tim wrote that the purpose of the research was to "determine the conditions under which psilocybin can be used to broaden and deepen human experience; to determine which persons are benefited by the drug, and in which direction; and to determine methods of making the beneficial effects durable and recoverable without subsequent exposure to the chemical." Despite the bad trips he had already seen and the undeniable fact that no procedures for choosing subjects had been established, Tim wrote, "The selection procedures assure that the need for using an antidote in one of our group sessions is probably less than the need for an antidote at a large cocktail party." Tim closed his letter by noting that he would be glad to answer any questions as well as make summary data about the research available if requested.

On November 26, Tim gave psilocybin to the poet Allen Ginsberg and his lover, Peter Orlovsky. Ginsberg had already taken peyote, mescaline, and LSD in the same Stanford University hospital where the novelist Ken Kesey first experienced the drug. Having come to Boston to address the Group for the Advancement of Psychiatry, Ginsberg read from his poems "Laughing Gas," "Mescaline," and "Lysergic Acid," all soon to be published in Kaddish and Other Poems, during his talk. The reaction was less than positive. The younger psychiatrists dismissed Ginsberg as clinically insane. The older psychiatrists, Freudians, told the poet that he had suffered a complete disintegration of the ego structure, descended into the id, and then re-created and integrated his ego in slightly changed form. Only Humphry Osmond seemed to understand what Ginsberg was talking about. Osmond and a colleague suggested that Ginsberg might want to meet a psychologist at Harvard who was working with a grant from Sandoz Laboratories.

After he returned to New York City, Ginsberg wrote the psychologist a letter, saying he would be honored to participate in the experiment. One week later, Tim knocked at Ginsberg's door. Although the poet was impressed that a Harvard professor would come all the way to the East Village just to see him.

Portions of Chapter 12 – Timothy Leary, A Biography, Robert Greenfield

Ginsberg in the introduction to 'High Priest' by Timothy Leary, published five years after the project was shutdown in 1963 writes:

The new consciousness born in these States can be traced back through old gnostic texts, visions, artists, and shamans; it is the consciousness of our ground nature suppressed and desecrated. It was always the secret tale of the tribe in America, this great scandal of the closing of the doors of perception of the Naked Human Form Divine. It began with the white murder of Indian inhabitants of the ground, the theft and later usurious exploitation of their land, it continued with an assault on all races and species of Mother Nature herself and concludes today with total disruption of the ecology of the entire planet. No wonder black slaves kept for non-human use into this century in tear-gassed ghettos of megalopolis were the first Aliens to sound the horn of Change, the first Strangers to Call the Great Call through Basilides' many Heavens. Amazing synchronism again, that Mr. Frank Takes Gun, Native American Church amerindian Peyote

155

Chief, invited the brilliantly talkative silver-haired psychiatrist who directed a Saskatchewan mental hospital in the 1940's to participate in a Peyote ritual, and that same Dr. Humphrey Osmond having recognized a wonder of consciousness thus experienced passed on the catalyst in Mescaline synthetic form to Aldous Huxley; and that Huxley's 1945 essay on the chemical opening of the Doors of Perception found its way to the tables of Bickford's Cafeteria Times Square New York, the couches of Reed College and Berkeley, where artist persons, having heard the Great Call of the African American, already initiated themselves en masse to subtle gradations of their own consciousness experienced while smoking the same Afric hemp smoked by Charles Parker Thelonious Monk 8 Dizzy Gillespie.

Dr. Timothy Leary takes up his part of the tale of the tribe in a Mexican hut and brings his discovery to Harvard harmoniously—and there begins the political battle, black and white magic become public visible for a generation. Dr. Leary is a hero of American consciousness. He began as a sophisticated academician, he encountered discoveries in his field which confounded him and his own technology, he pursued his studies where attention commanded, he arrived beyond the boundaries of public knowledge. One might hesitate to say, like Socrates, like Galileo?—poor Dr. Leary, poor Earth! Yet here we are in Science Fiction History, in the age of Hydrogen Bomb Apocalypse, the very Kali Yuga wherein man's stupidity so overwhelms the planet that ecological catastrophe begins to rehearse old tribes-tales of Karmaic retribution, Fire and Flood and Armageddon impending.

The Concord Prison Experiment

Aerial view of Concord Correctional Institute

During the period when psilocybin sessions were relocated to Newton House, Dr. Madison Presnell, a psychiatrist at a local prison, was invited to participate in a private session. Afterward, Timothy Leary had the opportunity to meet Dr. Presnell, and with his growing interest in applying psychological methods within the broader community, Leary decided to visit the prison. Accompanied by his colleague Frank Barron, he met with the prison's warden.

Barron later recalled the encounter, saying, "The warden was a tough but sincere Irish cop. He took one look at us—Francis Xavier Barron and Timothy Francis Leary—but he was genuine. He wanted to reduce the recidivism rate and said, 'Try anything. We can't seem to do a thing.'"

Since the psilocybin pills required medical approval, the future of the project depended heavily on the prison psychiatrist's consent.

Dr. Madison Presnell

The fate of the project hinged on the approval of a prison psychiatrist. In a prison hospital that Tim had been working in he met the dapper Dr. Madison Presnell, the first black psychiatrist he had ever encountered. Presnell told Tim that insofar as prisoners were concerned, their unconscious was their conscious mind and vice versa. They would never let people know how sensitive they were, that they liked poetry, could cry over a child, liked to see roses, or loved to walk through an open field. But when it came to their sex lives, a subject most people would never discuss, prisoners would lay it out from A to Z. Subjects that society at large believed should be hidden and forbidden, these men would talk about freely and openly. But anything "personal" was off limits. Presnell also told Tim that all his attempts to help them readjust to society had proven futile.

158

As Tim would later write, Presnell said, "If I could shatter that resistance, if I could just make them totally psychotic, I could cure them. I can cure psychotics but not severe neurotics because they are too conscious. If I could just get them to hear voices and see things and be so helpless and desperate that I could lead them back out of their desperation. But they're too suspicious and too knowledgeable." Tim told Presnell he had the drug that could do all this and more.

On Sunday, March 13, 1961, Presnell took psilocybin in Tim's house with his wife, Gunther Weil and his wife, and Ralph Metzner and his girlfriend. Metzner had already asked Tim whether he could be part of the prison project. Tim's first reaction was that Metzner was "too academic, too dainty-British, too bookish, too ivory tower, to walk into a prison and roll up his sleeves" to take a drug that would "put him out of his mind, with rough and tumble prisoners." Tim changed his opinion when Metzner told him that he was ready to do a session right then and there. By this point, Tim had already taken psilocybin fifty-one times. While Susan sat upstairs in her bedroom watching a John Wayne movie on television, the session began. Every time Presnell closed his eyes, he went someplace else. One moment, he was skiing down a snow-covered slope in Chile, the next he was on Copacabana beach in Rio de Janeiro. In an interview conducted by Peter Owen Whitmer, Presnell would later recall, "I said, 'When I close my eyes, I travel.' And that's really where the word 'trip' came from."

After taking psilocybin, Presnell returned to the prison to ask for volunteers for the study. Tim and his colleagues were about to put their theories on the line, but very stiff. It was very hard to break into his heart. At times in psychedelic sessions, I saw Ralph really collapse and cry like a baby like we all did. But it was rare to see that with him."

Concerned about what might happen when the research became part of the broader culture, Weil kept asking what he called "the Talmudic question": "What are we doing here? Is this right, or wrong?" In March, his question was answered by what came to be known as the Concord Prison Project. It

159

began when Tim found a note in his box at Harvard, informing him that two men from the Department of Legal Medicine were interested in enlisting the university's help in the psychological rehabilitation of prisoners. "Prison work is considered to be the least interesting, lowest status work you can do in the field of psychology, psychiatry, and sociology," Tim would later write. "The problems are hopeless. Criminals never change. The atmosphere is dreary and the academic rewards are slim." Nonetheless, the request was exactly what he had been looking for. Tim had already given mushroom pills to about a hundred people in "a wide variety of circumstances." His real problem was one that every coach had to face sooner or later: in order to find out if he was winning, Tim needed to come up with a way to keep score. Otherwise, there would be no empirical proof that the drug could not only bring people ecstasy but also educate and transform them. The prison system could provide him with an iron-clad statistic known as the recidivism, or return, rate. At that time, the recidivism rate in the Massachusetts state prison system was around 70 percent.

A week later, Tim Leary sat at a corner table at the Faculty Club with two officials from the state prison system who wanted to see Harvard graduate students assigned to the prisons as interns. Tim agreed to get Harvard to do this. In return, the officials agreed that if he could get the approval of the warden and the prison psychiatrist at the Massachusetts Correctional Institute at Concord, an antiquated institution not all that far from Cambridge which, as Tim would later write, looked like "Frankenstein made it," he could then give psychedelic mushrooms to prisoners.

The project ran from February 1961 until January 1963

In the Concord Prison Experiment, the idea was to use psilocybin to stimulate insight and behavioral changes in convicts and to see whether over the long term the intervention reduced the recidivism rate, which in the state prison system was around 70 percent. If it worked, it would be a great boon to society.

160

Convicts frequently are offered earlier release in exchange for volunteering for a study by some drug company. Tim didn't want to do that. It was inappropriate for what we were trying to accomplish. His attitude was, "We have found these experiences very interesting. We want to share them with you. In fact, we're going to experience them along with you. " That way, there could be trust right from the beginning.

It was a six-week program, with two psychedelic sessions—one at the start and one near the end. Most of the inmates were nearing release. The sessions took a group therapy format, with four or five inmates. The guides for the sessions were our graduate students from the Department of Social Relations, including Ralph Metzner, who signed up immediately, and Gunther Weil. Sometimes the inmates took the drugs under the supervision of the grad students; sometimes the grad students took the drugs too. Sometimes they exchanged roles, and the prisoners acted as guides. This reinforced trust. We administered psychological tests before and after.

Being Ram Dass, portions of Chapter 7

A total of 34 inmates participated in the rehabilitation project which has been in operation since March 1961. The program as now developed consists of six weeks of bi-weekly discussion meetings in small groups of three or four men, with two to three all-day psilocybin sessions. The purpose of the discussions is to assist inmates to integrate their experience into ordinary life and to help prepare them for the abrupt transition from prison to the street. Comparisons of personality test (CPI, MMPI) changes with pre-post differences in the control group showed significant increases in many scales (especially "responsibility," "socialization," tolerance," and "achievement"). There is also evidence for institutional work reports that inmates who have participated in the program make better impression on officers than those who have not.

Seven inmates have shown great interest in participating more actively in the program. While in the prison they act as assistant group leaders for new groups. Outside they help establish contacts for the Half-Way House.

The Halfway House, to be known as "Freedom Center" will provide assistance, in seeking employment, a meeting place, and possibly temporary living quarters for men when they are released. We are in contact with several real estate agents who are attempting to locate a suitable facility. Our legal adviser, Attorney Edward Ginsburg of Boston, is at present drawing up a charter to incorporate "Freedom Center." He has also consented to serve on the Board of Advisors.

Portions of Chapter 12 – Timothy Leary, A Biography, Robert Greenfield

The First Public Presentation

14th Annual Congress of Applied Psychology

Copenhagen, 1961

163

Leary and the Huxleys at the 14th Annual Congress of Applied Psychology, Copenhagen, Aug. 1961 Original: Leary Archives, NY Public Library.

Dear Aldous:

Our work is progressing well. A great interest is developing – mixed feelings generated-but on the whole I am most optimistic.

Professor Murray of Harvard has asked me to round you out in regard to addressing the XIV International Congress of Applied Psychology in Copenhagen – sometime between August 13-19 this summer.

I am chairman of a symposium which will take up (in part) the effeects of psychiatric drugs. Mr. Gerhart Nielsen is going to write you, not about this symposium but a general address to the entire conference. Hope you can come, - it would be fun to see you in Tivoli.

Dr. Hoffman wrote a most supportive lett(e)r-coming out decisively on the humanistic side. Mr. Gerald Herad also wrote co(n)mcering the Unitarian Seminary. Alan Watts has agreed to run the sessions and I hope this will start in March.

In regards to Copenhagen meeting you will hear from Nielsen in the near future.

Best Regards to Laura and yourself,

Sincerely,

Timothy Leary

Timothy Leary (l.), Richard Alpert (r.), Copenhagen 1961

The Paper Presented

Leary's First Article on Psilocybin

How to Change Behavior

Timothy Leary

"It is my plan to talk to you tonight about methods of effecting change—change in man's behavior and change in man's consciousness. Behavior and consciousness. Please note the paired distinction. Behavior and consciousness. Up until recently I considered myself a behavioral scientist and limited the scope of my work to overt and measurable behavior. In so doing I was quite in the Zeitgeist of modern psychology, studying the subject matter which our American predecessors defined some fifty years ago, behavior, routinely following the ground rules they laid down, scrupulously avoiding that which is most important to the subject—his consciousness, concentrating instead, on what is most important to we who seek to observe, measure, manipulate, control and predict—the subject's overt behavior. This decision to turn our backs on consciousness is, of course, typically western and very much in tune with the experimental, objective bent of Western science." - Timothy Leary's talk - <u>read more >>></u>

HOW TO CHANGE BEHAVIOR*

Timothy Leary
Harvard University

It is my plan to talk to you tonight about methods of effecting change--change in man's behavior and change in man's consciousness.

Behavior and Consciousness. Please note the paired distinction. Behavior and Consciousness. Up until recently I considered myself a behavioral scientist and limited the scope of my work to overt and measurable behavior. In so doing I was quite in the Zeitgeist of modern psychology. Studying the subject matter which our American predecessors defined some fifty years ago. Behavior. Routinely following the ground rules they laid down. Scrupulously avoiding that which is most important to the subject--his consciousness. Concentrating instead, on what is most important to we who seek to observe, measure, manipulate, control and predict--the subject's overt behavior.

The beginning of the typewritten script delivered at the Copenhagen talk.

Timothy Leary's "How to Change Behavior" was presented at the International Congress of Applied Psychology in Copenhagen in August of 1961, and was also reprinted in David Solomon's *LSD: The Consciousness-Expanding Drug* (1964). Leary had organized the plenary session of the International Congress; it included several distinguished speakers, including the novelist Aldous Huxley, Frank Barron of U.C. Berkeley, Richard Alpert and Henry A. Murray of Harvard, and himself. Each speaker was also an advocate of consciousness-expanding drugs. Psilocybin—synthesized magic mushrooms—was the drug of choice in 1961.

"How to Change Behavior" was Leary's first full-length article after his famous virginal experience with Mexican mushrooms in Cuernavaca in August of 1960 and as such, this article represents his first major work on psychedelics. Leary wanted a big stage for his presentation because he had a controversial message: a symbolic break with behaviorism, the dominant paradigm in applied psychology in the early 1960s. In this article, Leary notes that behaviorism is predicated on the "subject-object model" that attempts ". . . to observe, measure, manipulate, control, and predict —the subject's overt behavior." In place of behaviorism, Leary proposes a radical new paradigm: behavior change through consciousness-expanding drugs.

168

The crack within the department widened further that August, when Tim, Frank Barron, and I traveled to Copenhagen for the Fourteenth International Congress of Applied Psychology. We were scheduled to speak at one of the opening sessions, as was Aldous Huxley, before a gathering of professionals from all over the world. Before our lecture, I caused an inadvertent stir by attending a party with some Danish journalists and sharing some psilocybin so they could understand the research I was describing. My photo appeared in the newspaper with a headline about the crazy Harvard professor who was distributing poisonous drugs.

This caused consternation among psychologists at the convention. Their shock only grew when Tim lectured about the potential of psychedelics to cut through the "game" of Western life and change human behavior and consciousness. I spoke about the value of the inner journey—how psychedelics were worth investigating for their visionary qualities alone. Their mystical insights, I said, could produce love and peace.

Love and peace and personal growth are not the stuff of conventional scientific inquiry. Some attendees told Tim we'd set Danish psychology back twenty years. People wondered what on earth was going on at Harvard.

The conference was our first public declaration of the promise we saw in psychedelics for real change. On the one hand, it brought us attention.

Portions of Chapter 7, Being Ram Dass, Rameshwar Das

After Copenhagen – "The Fall Out"

The New York Times

TUESDAY, MAY 13, 1952

Lamont Named Fellow Of Harvard Corporation

Thomas S. Lamont

Thomas S. Lamont

Special to THE NEW YORK TIMES.

CAMBRIDGE, Mass., May 12 —Thomas S. Lamont of New York, vice president of J. P. Morgan & Company, was elected today to the seven-man corporation of Harvard University.

The Harvard Corporation consists of the president and treasurer of Harvard University, serving ex officio, and five fellows elected for life. As a fellow of Harvard College Mr. Lamont succeeds Henry L. Shattuck of Boston, senior member of the corporation, who has retired after twenty-three years of service.

Mr. Shattuck was treasurer of Harvard from 1929 until 1938, when he was elected a fellow. The major actions of the corporation are subject to review by the thirty-man Board of Overseers, elected by the alumni.

Mr. Lamont served as an overseer from 1945 to 1951. He is president of the Board of Trustees of Phillips Exeter Academy and a trustee of the Carnegie Foundation for the Advancement of Teaching and of the Academy of Political Science.

171

It was a sign of things to come when Timothy Leary decided to visit Gordon Wasson's apartment in New York City. As we made our way through the bustling streets, Tim filled me in on Wasson's impressive background. A Columbia School of Journalism graduate turned financial writer, Wasson eventually worked for J.P. Morgan. "Sandoz was a client," Tim explained. "That's how Wasson became a director. I keep him in the loop about everything we're doing. I need his guidance—Sandoz has poured money into psilocybin research and hasn't seen a single return on investment. And Wasson, well, he knows that better than anyone. He's a banker. But in other ways, he's further out than any of us. Wait till you read his stuff."

I couldn't help but anticipate reading the mushroom book that George Andrews had mentioned in his letter. Tonight, I suspected my role was simply to reassure Wasson that I had "made it" in the community, even though he, of all people, must have understood that mushrooms weren't just for counterculture figures and criminals. I dressed the part—blazer, slacks, shirt, and tie—while Tim opted for his usual tweed jacket, exuding the air of a professor.

We arrived at One East End Avenue, a prestigious prewar co-op with views of the East River, and were directed to Wasson's apartment. When he opened the door, he was a surprising sight: blue button-down shirt, tan Bermuda shorts, sandals without socks. "Far out," Tim had said earlier, and now I understood what he meant—Wasson was anything but the suit-and-tie figure I had expected. Despite his casual attire, his stocky build and sharp gaze revealed a man in control. He greeted us with a handshake, though his eyes appeared distant.

Tim wasted no time introducing me as someone who could support psilocybin research, but Wasson cut straight to the point. "Well, Dr. Leary, what happened in Stockholm?" he asked, referring to the medical convention in July, where hallucinogenic drugs had been discussed.

172

"We had some trouble there," Tim admitted with a smile. "There was a lot of interest, but the press was difficult. The Communist paper said we were using mushrooms for capitalist propaganda to spread religion. Then, I gave an interview where a reporter misquoted me, saying that if Kennedy and Khrushchev took mushrooms, it would end the Cold War."

Wasson raised an eyebrow. "I thought you believed that. You didn't say it?"

"Not in those words," Tim clarified. "Things got worse when another reporter asked Dick Alpert if he could try psilocybin, and Dick let him."

"Gave him psilocybin?" Wasson's voice sharpened.

"Yes, it might have been a mistake," Tim admitted. "The article came out flippant, like the reporter didn't take the drug seriously."

Wasson, lips pressed tightly together, remained unresponsive. When Tim offered to send him the articles, Wasson simply nodded. Then Tim pushed harder, trying to win him over. "We want to give mushrooms to everyone who wants them. Sandoz has been generous, but the two thousand pills a month that were enough last year are no longer enough. We know you've invested millions in psilocybin and LSD research, and we're not asking for subsidies forever. We want to form a research foundation, led by eminent people. People like Huxley, Heard... and yourself."

Tim paused, expecting Wasson to be flattered and eager to join the cause. But there was only silence. Wasson said nothing.

In retrospect, it became clear that this meeting with Wasson was the first real warning that the psilocybin project was on shaky ground. Recently, Leary and Aldous Huxley had gone to Copenhagen for an international congress of psychologists. Both had spoken about psilocybin, but indiscreet interviews given by Leary and Richard Alpert had caused a stir in the press. Alpert had once again offered the drug to journalists during an interview, and the scandal that followed was hard to ignore.

The situation had not gone unnoticed at Harvard either. Rumors circulated that the administration was preparing to take action. Wasson, a careful and measured man, seemed well aware of the danger. In a letter, he later expressed his concern, suggesting that any drastic action from Harvard could backfire. "Leary might enjoy a story in the papers about his experiments being stopped by the authorities," Wasson warned, his voice tinged with suspicion. "He enjoys the limelight, even if it costs him his job."

It was becoming increasingly clear that the enthusiasm of Leary and his colleagues, while well-intentioned, was leading them toward a collision with forces beyond their control. Sandoz might have been willing to fund research, but the Harvard authorities were less forgiving. The fate of the project—and perhaps Leary's career—was hanging by a thread.

'The' Letter

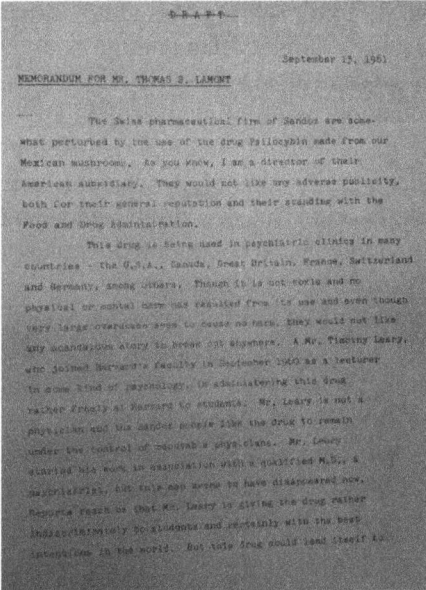

September 15, 1961

Exposed

The Swiss pharmaceutical firm of Sandoz are somewhat perturbed by the use of the drug Psilocybin made from our Mexican mushrooms. As you know, I am a director of their American subsidiary. They would not like any adverse publicity, both for their general reputation and their standing with the Food and Drug Administration

This drug is being used in psychiatric clinics in many countries – the U.S.A., Canada, Great Britain, France, Switzerland and Germany, among others. Though it is not toxic and- no physical or mental harm has resulted from its use and even though very large overdoses seem to causa no harm,

175

they would not like any scandalous story to break out anywhere. A Mr. Timothy Leary, who joined Harvard's faculty in September i960 as a lecturer In some kind of psychology, is administering this drug rather freely at Harvard to students. Mr. Leary is not a physician and the Sandoz people like the drug to remain under the control of reputable physicians. Mr. Leary started his work in association with a qualified M.D., a psychiatrist, but this man seems to have disappeared now. Reports reach us that Mr. Leary is giving the drug rather indiscriminately to students and certainly with the best Intentions in the world. But this drug could lend itself to sensational stories, as you can imagine. We are thinking of not acceding to Mr. Leary's request for a further supply. Incidentally, Aldous Huxley, a first-class writer and a personage in the English-speaking world, is associated with these experiments. He has been in Harvard in the spring term. Recently Leary and Huxley went to Copenhagen, to an international congress of psychologists, where they both spoke about Psilocybin and where indiscreet interviews given by Leary and another associate, whose name I do not know, caused considerable furor in the Copenhagen press. This unnamed colleague gave the drug to two of the journalists who were interviewing him.

I understand that the authorities at Harvard are alive to the situation and they may well be on the point of taking measures. I would be loath to do anything that would harm Timothy Leary whose Intentions are certainly of the finest, and I should certainly not wish either myself or Sandoz to be associated with any step you might take. You will, I know, be tactful in broaching the subject and learning what the situation in Cambridge is. I think any violent action might very easily be unwise. Leary might possibly like a story to break in the papers about his experiments with the drug and action by the authorities I stopping this. I fancy he is somewhat inclined to enjoy the lime¬light, even if it costs him his job. A tactful approach to him suggesting that he associate himself with a qualified M.D. would be helpful all around.

R. Gordan Wasson

Request to Sandoz

November 21, 1961 Leary writes a letter to Sandoz asking for more. By this time Sandoz has been alerted to their 'unscientific activities'.

November 14, 1961

Carl Henze, M. D.
Sandoz Laboratory
Medical Department
Hanover, New Jersey

Dear Doctor Henze:

Thanks for your letter of November 9th asking about our future psilocybin research.

As you know we have completed a large naturalistic study of the effects of the drug in supportive environment. The results on over 250 subjects have been IBM processed and are being written up by George Litwin and myself. These data suggest that if psilocybin is given in a serious, collaborative, non-laboratory environment the experience is almost always pleasant and very often dramatically insightful. Our evidence compels the conclusion that valuable potentialities for human welfare exist.

In the spring of 1961 we began to study the issue of application. How should psilocybin be best employed. At that time we began the prisoner rehabilitation project and an individual therapy project. The results of these "behavior change" studies are now being tabulated by Miss Sara Kinne, a Harvard graduate student, and a preliminary analysis has shown dramatic changes on personality tests.

Our naturalistic and behavior change studies have attracted the interest of many local scientists. The psilocybin research team now includes four faculty members (Leary, Alpert, Presnell and Kahn of Yale) and seven graduate students (Litwin, Metzner, Weil, Schwitzgebel, Clark, Kinne, Berger). Over twenty five more faculty members and graduate students have asked to join our research projects.

Because of this growing interest in our project and, further, because of the eagerness of many participants to change their professional career plans in order to remain on our project we decided to consider a more formal administration.

On October 8th a planning meeting was held. In addition to our staff the following people were present:

Professor David C. McClelland, Ph. D.
Professor Huston Smith, Ph. D.
Professor John Spiegel, M. D.
Arnold Abrams, M. D.
Donnell Boardman, M. D.
Gerald Klerman, M. D.

177

George Keefe, parole officer
Mary Maher, parole officer
Dr. Raymond Gilbert, Deputy Commissioner of Correction
Dr. Walter Clark, Ph. D.

The consensus of this meeting was that this research was very exciting and should definitely be continued, but that a more formal administration was called for.

It was recommended that a smaller advisory board be set up to work out details for research administration.

The committee which met a week later consisted of Alpert, Klerman, Leary, McClelland and Spiegel. At this meeting it was formally agreed that we should aim our efforts in two directions: (a) the continuation of research projects on psilocybin experience and behavior change to be carried on within the University, and (b) the development and maintenance of an independent foundation in the community for other aspects of our program. At this time we also considered the plan for the appraisal of new research within the University program. It was agreed that a permanent advisory board be set up for this purpose.

Dr. Leary and Dr. Alpert subsequently met with Professor Robert White, Chairman of the Department of Social Relations. Dr. White gave strong support to our program and urged us to continue. The political-legal issues were discussed. In order to provide protection to all concerned -- Harvard, the members of our group and pharmaceutical companies with whom we work -- it was agreed that we should approach Dr. Dana Farnsworth, Director of the University Health Services, and a psychiatrist of high repute in the community.

On November 2nd, Drs. Leary and Alpert met with Dr. Farnsworth and presented the entire picture to him. After a thorough review of the many aspects of doing drug research within the university community, we requested that Dr. Farnsworth's staff provide (a) medical screening for our staff and subjects, and (b) on call psychiatric service during our sessions. Dr. Farnsworth readily agreed to both of these requests and urged that we proceed with our work at Harvard.

We are, of course, delighted with the program as it now stands and the support and understanding provided by the chairman of the Department of Social Relations and the director of the Harvard Health Services gives us and you solid social-legal protection.

We are now proceeding with three large research studies:

1. Prisoner Rehabilitation
2. Assessment of Growth Experience and Personality Change
3. Studies of Alteration of Perceptual Processes

All subjects will undergo a physical examination and psychiatric screening, and there will be medical-psychiatric coverage of all sessions.

In addition to these Harvard programs we are considering plans for an independent foundation. We shall keep you informed of our plans as they develop.

178

Doctor C. Henze -3-

     Last summer we discussed with you the broad educational, religious and social implications of conscious-expanding substances. Each week finds prominent and competent people offering to join these activities. We are proceeding with ever greater investments of time and personnel and we are eager to receive your reactions to our plans.

     The next series of research and rehabilitation groups is scheduled to begin on November 20th. Would you please send us 2,000 tablets by that date? We are now arranging for medical clearance for the subjects and sessions involved. Dr. Alpert and I hope to come to Hanover in the near future to talk with you about our work and the important part Sandoz can take in it.

     Thanks again for your interest and help. Dr. Alpert joins me in sending warm wishes to you and Dr. Gimbel.

                                        Sincerely yours,

                                        Timothy Leary

TL:pc

The Walls Were Beginning to Crack

We had some support at Harvard, most notably from Henry Murray, the former director of the Harvard Psychological Clinic, who volunteered to try psilocybin. Many of our other departmental colleagues, however, were starting to harbor doubts about our research. Stories were flying around campus about our sessions with artists and flamboyant musicians and about graduate students taking drugs. Though our methodology involved reporting on internal states and subjective experiences, Tim and I believed we could show demonstrable effects on creativity, as well as therapeutic benefits and religious or mystical experiences.

Dave McClelland and other faculty members didn't buy it. In their view, scientific data had to be objectively verifiable, which is hard when you are talking about highly subjective internal experiences. Objective knowledge must be repeatable so that it can be studied by more than one person; what we were doing, said our colleagues, was self-validating our work. Behaviorism was still paramount for many of the psychologists at Harvard. A good scientist observed measurable changes in behavior, designing rigorous protocols, testing rats in labyrinths, and collecting data.

But you couldn't use rats to explore awareness. Our research wasn't about measuring every little behavior—it was about life-altering experience. Our colleagues didn't accept this paradigm. The psilocybin project staff would gather at lunchtime in the library of the Center for Research in Personality and discuss our trips, trying to develop language for them. Lunchtime began to be noticeably divided between those who were in the psilocybin project and those who were not.

This only exacerbated the growing rift between us and the other faculty. It wasn't just about scientific methodology. Our research was attracting more graduate students, leaving other professors with fewer assistants to run surveys and experiments. The psilocybin project was the most exciting thing happening.

180

On a stop in London after the conference, for example, we tripped with the novelist William Burroughs, who enjoyed the experience so much that he flew to the US and moved into Tim's house temporarily to participate in our research. Burroughs had famously killed his wife in an accident trying to shoot an apple off her head like William Tell, and he was an acerbic character. He'd tried all sorts of drugs; if there was ever someone who knew about pharmacology from the inside, it was him.

Our stance made people in the Harvard scientific community nervous. When we returned, Dave distributed a memo at one of our faculty meetings in which he outlined his growing concern. "Many reports are given of deep mystical experiences," he wrote, "but their chief characteristic is the wonder at one's own profundity." He wanted fewer subjective reports and more control and hard data.

"I had already become a controversial figure around the Boston area, because everything that I was saying made a tremendous amount of sense to students and patients, but the doctors, the psychiatrists, the social workers, the professors, the psychologists, were not so quick to accept these theories."

High Priest - pp. 174-189

During the fall and the winter of 1960, much of my me and energy was going into the study of the effects of the psychedelic mushrooms. I was also carrying on an active program of lecturing, teaching, and field work in clinical psychology in the Harvard Graduate School. I had been brought to Harvard in 1959 in order to introduce existential-transactional methods for behavior change. After fifteen years of practicing psychotherapy and about ten years of doing research on psychotherapy, I had come to the conclusion that there was very little that one person called a doctor could do for anther person called a patient by talking to him across a desk, or listening to him as he lay on a couch. I developed a lot of theories and a lot of methods on how behavior change could be brought bout more effectively than the standard clinical interview method.

There are two main points to the theories I developed; first (transactional) I was convinced that the doctor had to suspend his or her role and status as a doctor, had to join the other person actively and collaboratively in figuring out the solution to his problem. As much as possible, the doctor had to turn over the responsibility to the man who knew most about the problem at hand, namely, the patient. I developed many techniques for getting patients to help each other.

The second point in my theory (existential) was that the doctor has to leave the safety of his consulting room and get out there in the field where the so-called patient is having his unique problems, and here he is going to solve his problems. I saw the role of the doctor as that of a coach in a game in which the patient was the star player. The coach can help, can point out mistakes, can share his wisdom, but in the last analysis, the guy who does the job is the guy out there in the field, the so-called patient.

I was enthusiastic about these theories because they worked, and because no joy in teaching can equal that thrill which comes when you watch someone who's been hung up, and blocked, and confused, and making a mess of things out there in the field suddenly learn how. All this had started happening before I got involved in the drug research, and I had already become a controversial figure around the Boston area, because everything that I was saying made a tremendous amount of sense to students and patients, but the doctors, the psychiatrists, the social workers, the professors, the psychologists, were not so quick to accept these theories. I was asking them to give up the status and the omniscient position which they felt their training entitled them to. I asked them to turn over the authority and the star role in the game to the patient.

Lurking in the Darkness

On the Monday after my psilocybin trip, I showed up on campus to deliver a scheduled lecture for the class Social Relations 143, Human Motivation. As I began, I felt distracted. I wanted to share what had happened on Saturday. The problem was, there was nothing in any psychology textbook that described my experience. I knew my students could benefit, but I had no context—no terminology, no academic explanation—from which to communicate that ineffable new sense of self. This planted some doubts about psychology. If my psilocybin experience was true, then everything I was teaching about motivational psychology was utterly beside the point. I was teaching stuff, and my students were writing it all down, but the disparity between realities— between my consciousness on Saturday night and my professorial explanations on Monday morning—was disconcerting. I felt guilty. Was I being a complete hypocrite? Psychologists think that reality is ultimately psychological, and yet the psilocybin trip had shown me that I was more than a psychological entity. Until that moment, the only stirring of my spirit had been in Quaker meetings at Wesleyan. Now, I knew from my own experience there was another plane of consciousness beyond time and space.

After two or three more days, I was talking about the psilocybin trip in the past tense. My personality patterns kept infiltrating my newly liberated mind, old thought habits sneakily reasserting themselves. The material realities of classes and meetings and groceries intruded once again. The pure white of the blizzard melted into piles of dirty snow. Neurotic old Richard was back.

Still, even though I was back in my psychological self, my thinking mind and ego, I was different. The roles—professor, son, pilot, cellist—returned, but I didn't identify with them in the same way. The observer stance I'd long cultivated had new meaning. There was a way to observe life from this quiet center within, from the soul. I'd tasted a reality where I was

183

home in my heart, and even the memory—that lightness of pure being—remained with me.

And yet. I knew I didn't fully know, at least not in a way I could explain to my students. I had worked so hard to become a member of the academic community, and now I felt disconnected. Everyone assumed I knew things because I was a Harvard professor. But I didn't know about this, and when I listened to my colleagues, I realized they didn't either. These were lions of academia, at the apex of Western learning. We were all enjoying the world of our own thought forms. We were fascinated by our theories. We were all going on about the workings of the mind.

But we didn't have wisdom. The awareness behind it all, the consciousness that moves it all, was a mystery.

Richard Alpert, March 6, 1961

David McClelland at Radcliff - 1961

Notes to the Psilocybin Team

Psilocybin Research Project

by David McClelland.

(October 1961, One month after Copenhagen)

Since the reports of the effects of the psilocybin have been largely subjective, it may be helpful in planning future research. To try and summarize here what some of the effects of participating in the project seem to be as seen by outsiders, that is the drug alters consciousness dramatically. But a further interesting question not directly touched on in the recent report of these studies is whether this alteration affects a person's relation to reality or his interpersonal relationships. Hence, a summary of

185

these effects as very imperfectly observed from the outside may be helpful. Though it is made obviously on the basis of very scanty data and under the influence of pressures that always exist against innovations that break sharply with tradition or social usage. New to begin with, psilocybin and similar substances have been around a long time, and we should be able to learn something of their possible social effects from observing other groups that have taken them in the past. To judge by the behavior of Mexican eros and Indian mystics, one would expect its chief effects to be one, to encourage withdrawal from contact with social reality. And two, to increase satisfaction with one's own inner thought life.

Actually, the descriptions of the effects of psilocybin as summarized by research reports from the current project are not inconsistent with these expectations. In more detail, the following effects have been noted. One, disassociation and detachment. From the subjective point of view, this appears apparently largely as a gain from the social point of view. It may be a negative feature initiatives bring to show a certain blandness or superiority or feeling of being above and beyond the normal world of social reality. They feel sorry for those who have not had the experience. Social rules, roles and regulations seem remote and slightly ridiculous. Everything is a game. All is illusion, even self. In other words, the inner world of fantasy is valued more than the outer world of social reality. Furthermore, this may be coupled with irritation at attempts to introduce reality testing that varies all the way from the simple resistance to introducing ordinary scientific or medical legal precautions to outright attacks on science and on the uninitiated who still believe in observing normal social rules and procedures.

The sharpest attacks from society on what has seemed occasionally to be developing artistically withdrawal now have produced a certain caution in promoting the wonders of the world of psilocybin. But this seems more a matter of strategy for Hammond handling those who don't comprehend rather than conviction that a hard realistic problem to be faced in using psilocybin is its tendency to encourage withdrawal from social world. It is

186

probably no accident that the society, which most consistently encouraged the use of these substances, India produce more or one of the sickest social orders ever created by mankind in which Thinking men spend their time lost in Buddha position under the influence of drugs, exploring consciousness while poverty, disease, social discrimination, and superstition reach their highest and most organized form in all history.

TO MARK A SPOT

Lisa Bieberman Kuenning, early undergraduate working in an administrative position with the program.

My favorite campus organization at this time was the Harvard Humanists, and its chief pleasure and reason for being was to disprove the existence of God and to debunk all religions. It was to this group that I proposed inviting Dr. Timothy Leary or Dr. Richard Alpert as a speaker. The suggestion was received with enthusiasm by the others, who may not have been much more single-minded in their rationalism than I.

A few days later I was standing in the office of Dr. Leary, requesting the man behind the desk to come and speak to the Harvard Humanists about his work with psilocybin. The middle-aged gentleman with the hearing aid attached by a cord to the floor said he would do it. But not this month; he hadn't the time. How about April? Well, I wanted him for a meeting in March. The first small tug of war between my impatience and his convenience, of dozens to come, was won, as it was always to be, by Leary. We scheduled him for April.

Another group was ahead of us. A sign in Emerson Hall announced that Dr. Leary would address the Soc Rel Colloquium on the *"Politics of Consciousness."* Though I had no connection with the *Soc Rel Colloquium*, a seminar for graduate students and faculty, I went to the meeting. To my intense pleasure, Dr. Leary recognized the girl who had stood in his office

187

and greeted me by name. I was still telling myself that my interest was impersonal.

By the time the meeting had ended, the pretense was smashed, never again to be restored; I had become an unashamed monomaniac desiring just one thing: to get some psilocybin and take it. I had expected more guardedness from Leary, more of the academic distance that professors I knew were accustomed to maintain. It electrified me to realize as he spoke, that he was as caught up in the mystical potentialities of psilocybin as ever I had been. His tone was that of a believer, but not unmixed with wit; it was almost conspiratorial. He spoke of how the mystical experience, from which we are cut off by the tyranny of the rational mind, had been the goal of all religions. How men had for centuries used sacred "vegetables" to attain this experience. (Even then Tim Leary had a defensive terminology. He avoided the word "drug.") How he himself had broken through the barrier in the blue sun of Mexico, by eating the sacred mushroom *teonanacatl*. How the guardians of the established conceptual scheme had always feared the divine revelation, and thus even now his research was hemmed about with restrictions and suspicion.

During the question period, I asked what were the legal restrictions on the sale of psilocybin; Dr. Leary laughed and said, "Well it's not for sale." Sandoz Company, the manufacturer, was supplying only research projects. My heart sank, for I knew that Harvard had barred Leary from using undergraduate subjects.

As the group was dispersing, another undergrad asked Leary whether there was any way he could take the mushroom drug. "You'll have to graduate or quit school" was the startling reply. Never before had I heard a teacher suggest to a student, even in such a hypothetical form as this, that he might quit school. Even with my intense desire for the experience, I was not ready to go that far. But could I wait for graduation, over a year away? Would Leary and his drugs still be around?

Working with Washington

Mr. John L. Harvey
Deputy Commissioner
Department of Health, Education, and Welfare
Food and Drug Administration
Washington 25, D. C.

Dear Mr. Harvey:

    Dr. Alpert and myself are most grateful to you and Dr. Kessenich for making possible our conversation with you on January 11th. We were most pleased at your immediate and accurate understanding of the issues involved in the complex area of consciousness-expanding drugs. We believe that a review of the major points raised would be helpful to all concerned.

Group Leaders

    There is, at present, a group of psychologists who, during the past year have become very familiar with psilocybin and its effects. They have each participated in a number of sessions both as member and leader. We start with this group as a nucleus of administrators. The group includes: Timothy Leary, Richard Alpert, Michael Kahn, George Litwin, Ralph Metzner, Gunther Weil, Ralph Schwitzgebel, Michael Hollingshead.

The Game Gets an Upgrade

"Like a high-voltage jolt, LSD changed the nature of the Psilocybin Project at Harvard. Psilocybin, as we'd experienced it, was a relational and unifying drug. The doses we administered were relatively small, six to eight milligrams, and the trips we guided lasted just three or four hours. Participants remembered their names and situations even as they reported feelings of oneness. Boundaries melted with a sense of warmth and understanding. Psilocybin softened the ego and opened the heart.

LSD blew all that away. It caused, not a softening of the ego, but its death."
- Being Ram Dass, p. 83

Mescalin and LSD

Invoice to Dr. Richard Alpert from L.Light & Co. LTD, Colnbrook, England for Mescaline. April 5, 1962.[/caption]

190

Mescaline

On the Genealogy of Mescaline (1887–1919) DEPT. DASTON
BETWEEN THE NATURAL AND THE HUMAN SCIENCES IVO
GURSCHLER According to Sasha Shulgin (*Alexander Shulgin, the most
prolific psychedelic chemist in history*), Mescaline has become the "meter"
for psychedelic substances, as it was the first of its kind to be approached
scientifically. But how did a Mexican cactus turn into a chemically pure
substance after all? In Berlin 1888, the toxicologist Louis Lewin published
his first analysis of a yet unidentified cactus, which he brought with him
from North America. Only later did it become clear that this was a
specimen of Peyote, which indigenous people have traditionally used and
worshipped as a spiritual vehicle.

LSD - *Lysergic acid diethylamide*

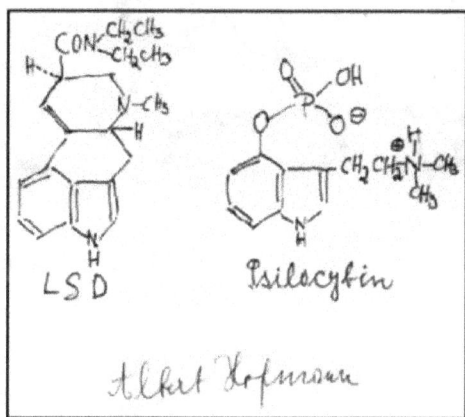

Albert Hofmann's laboratory journal illustrations of LSD and psilocybin.
Swedish chemist Albert Hofmann completed his doctoral work at the
University of Zurich in 1929, where he first demonstrated competency as
an accomplished plant and animal chemist.

191

The first shipment of LSD-25 to American researchers was received by a team headed by Max Rinkel at Boston Psychopathic Hospital, a clinic associated with Harvard University, in 1949-50 At the 1950 meeting of the American Psychiatric Association Rinkel announced results showing that LSD induced temporary psychotic episodes in normal subjects, setting forth hope that it would soon be possible to study mental disorders objectively in laboratory settings (Lee and Shlain, Acid Dreams, 20) Rinkel's team used a variety of strategies to measure the effects of LSD on 100 "normal" volunteers as well as on hospitalized psychiatric patients.

Sidney Cohen – LSD Experiments at the Veteran's Administration Hospital in Los Angeles Video Link:

https://youtu.be/glTB9vtNueQ

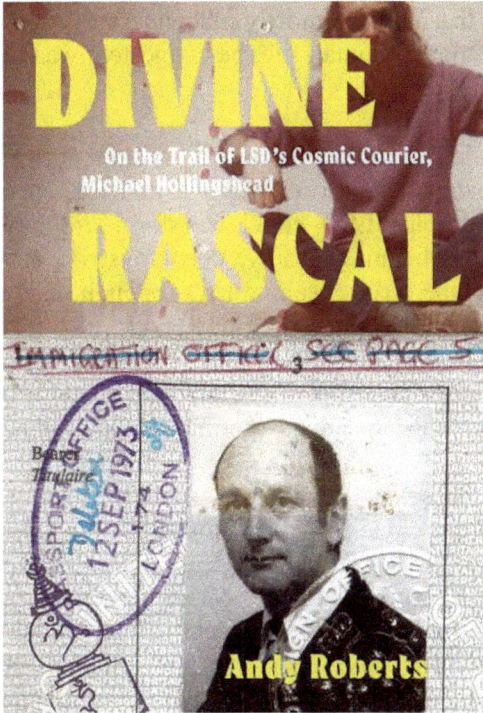

The Man Who Turned On the World, Michael Hollingshead

Michael Hollingshead introduced Timothy Leary to LSD in December 1961

Aldous Huxley was the obvious person to call. Given his experience with mescaline and LSD, he might have insight into the direction psychedelic research was taking. When I reached him, he was sympathetic but admitted that no one could yet say with certainty what LSD would reveal or where it would lead. What was clear, however, was the growing curiosity it stirred among those who had encountered it. He reflected on the idea that, at some level, people already sense the existence of an "Other World" within their own minds—an inner dimension that remains mostly hidden. Any serious discussion of its nature and relevance to human life, he suggested, was of universal significance.

Huxley speculated that psychedelics might be most effective when incorporated into a structured discipline—a kind of yoga of heightened awareness. Under the right conditions, LSD could transform ordinary reality into an experience of overwhelming beauty, deep mystery, and revelation. But he warned that the drug itself wasn't enough. True awareness required more than a chemical catalyst; it had to be cultivated through conscious engagement with life. Psychedelics, he proposed, might best be understood as a therapy for the widespread spiritual and perceptual dullness that modern psychology mislabeled as 'normality' or 'mental health.'

A few days later, Huxley called back. He had given my situation some thought and had a recommendation: I should go to Harvard and meet Dr. Timothy Leary. Huxley had met Leary earlier that year in Copenhagen, where Leary had presented a paper at the Fourteenth International Congress of Applied Psychology. His talk, *How to Change Behavior*, described the induction of visionary states through psilocybin, a synthetic form of Mexico's sacred mushroom. Huxley spoke highly of him—not just as a scientist but as a person. "A splendid fellow," he said, adding that Leary had written three major works on personality and psychotherapy.

"If there is anyone in America worth talking to about this," Huxley told me, "it's Dr. Leary."

That conversation led to my introduction to Leary, and soon after, I became deeply involved in the unfolding psychedelic movement. I was there for some of its defining moments, including the *Concord Prison Project* (1961–63), where Leary explored psilocybin's potential to reduce recidivism among inmates, and the *Good Friday Experiment* (1962), in which Harvard Divinity School students examined the spiritual effects of

194

psilocybin. These projects, and the broader movement they fueled, would shape the future of psychedelic research for decades to come.

Lysergic acid diethylamide (LSD) was made available by Sandoz Laboratory in Switzerland to research institutions, psychiatrists and physicians in 1947 under the trademark name, Delysid, for its potential in medicinal-psychiatric use. Playing the role of a drug aid in the context of psychoanalytic and psychotherapeutic treatment, LSD gained popularity in clinical treatment settings, notably by Ronald Sandison in European practice and Humphry Osmond in North America.

Frank Barron was the first to warn Leary to keep his discovery private. When he saw Leary organizing a large research project with graduate students, he was visibly unsettled. To Barron, this kind of exploration was deeply personal—something to be directly experienced rather than turned into an institutional study. "Take it yourself and read Blake," he told Leary. Barron had taken the mushrooms two years earlier, and the experience had plunged him into a year of wild poetry, deep contemplation, and the dedicated study of mystical philosophy.

The idea of subjecting such an intimate, transformative experience to academic bureaucracy made no sense to him. The politics, administration, and structure of a formal research program seemed completely at odds with what psychedelics were meant to reveal. Barron, a scholar of the old school—a mix of William James' philosophical depth and Dylan Thomas' poetic intuition—found the bureaucratic approach alienating. His Celtic mysticism had no patience for committee meetings and grant proposals. Studying the effects of sacred mushrooms within the framework of psychological research seemed to him absurd.

Trouble with the Faculty

PROF. HERBERT C. KELMAN

Herbert C. Kelman
Richard Clarke Cabot Professor of Social Ethics, Emeritus, Harvard
University

From the start, Harvard professor Herbert C. Kelman saw Timothy Leary as a disruptor in the field of psychology. Kelman had been familiar with Leary's earlier work, but when Leary arrived at Harvard, something had clearly changed. "He had gone through some kind of transition," Kelman later recalled. "He had become a bit Messianic and had all these ideas about how the field was being done the wrong way."

196

By the time Leary began teaching at Harvard, he had already started experimenting with hallucinogens. His first experience with psilocybin was in the summer of 1960, and soon after, he and Richard Alpert (later known as Ram Dass) incorporated psychedelics into their research, using graduate students as test subjects.

Kelman, who was in Norway when Leary arrived, first heard rumors of the experiments through letters from students. "There were hints about drugs and drug-taking," he said. But it wasn't until he returned to campus in the spring of 1962 that he started raising concerns in department meetings. However, David McClelland, then chair of the Department of Social Relations and director of the Center for Research in Personality, did not take immediate action.

The issue became harder to ignore when a student in Leary's course approached Kelman directly. The student was hesitant but eventually confided that students felt pressured to take psychedelics as part of the course. "It had become so legitimized in the eyes of the students that they felt like they had to do it," Kelman recalled.

Psychology professor Robert Rosenthal, who arrived at Harvard immediately after Leary's departure in 1963, confirmed that Leary had made psychedelic use central to his work. "He more or less made it a requirement to do psilocybin," Rosenthal said. "We regarded it as kind of shocking that he got away with as much as he did."

As the controversy grew and more students spoke up, Kelman confronted McClelland about Leary and Alpert distributing hallucinogens to students. With increasing public scrutiny, the research soon became impossible to ignore.

Why then do I object to the Psilocybin Program? I object to it because of the way in which these various activities - which in themselves are not objectionable and often, in fact, laudable - are carried out. I object to the atmosphere that surrounds the Psilocybin Program and to the general philosophy of which the taking of the Mexican mushroom is the primary symbolic expression. There are many specific points on which I could dwell - such as the non-dilatant attitude toward experimental controls and the equally non-dilatant attitude toward the effects of the drug on the subject - that seem to characterize the Psilocybin Program.

"Kelman was a formidable rival. He had undeniable clout in Washington, as demonstrated by an uncanny facility for obtaining annual grants, fellowships, and visiting professorships in foreign countries. Actually, no one could explain why he was in the Center for Personality Research since his field was social and political psychology. Richard and I knew that Kelman was preparing an ambush."

Flashbacks, pp. 119-122

The Beginning of the End

As the research was expanding at Harvard, there were other areas in the northeast that were also involved with these new mind-expanding substances. Allen Ginsberg, Jack Kerouac, Neal Cassidy, William Burroughs, Charles Olson, Arthur Koestler, Robert Lowell, Gerald Heard, Alan Watts, and Muriel Rukyser - to mention a few. Musicians also, Thelonious Monk and Dizzy Gillespie, met and had psilocybin sessions with Tim. It was during this early period:

The chairman of my department called me. What the hell is going on, Tim? Two graduate students have come to me indignant, demanding that your work be stopped. I laughed. I'll send you the reports from the session as soon as they are typed. It was a good session. We're learning a lot.

The disapproving gaze of the establishment was on us.

From this time on we saw ourselves as unwitting agents of a social process that was far too powerful for us to control or to more than dimly understand. - Timothy Leary

The Harvard Crimson

The University Daily Est. 1873

In February a Crimson article by Andrew Weil a newsletter was sent out.

'Better Than a Damn'

From the Bottle

By Andrew T. Weil

February 20, 1962

ANDREW THOMAS WEIL

1963

Here is a portion -

Investigators of psilocybin at Harvard's Center for Research In Personality are unbounded in their enthusiasm for this new drug, reporting that it frequently increases powers of creative thinking in both artistic and scientific areas. A number of authors (Aldous Huxley, William Burroughs, Allen Ginsberg, and others) studied in the Harvard project found that their work benefited enormously from the influence of psilocybin, and preliminary investigations have indicated that the "mushroom experience" may be of value in the rehabilitation of prisoners. The directors of the Center envision the use of psilocybin in a "mushroom seminar" for graduate students in theology, behavioral science, and philosophy, the course would be based on taking the drug once a month and spending the intervening sessions applying the insights gained to problems in the respective fields. - Harvard Crimson

EXPLAIN YOURSELF

The Psilocybin Project Newsletter #1, February 1962

Recently our Western science has provided, in the form of chemicals, the most direct techniques for opening new realms of awareness. William James used nitrous oxide and ether to "stimulate the mystical consciousness in an extraordinary degree." Today the attention of psychologists, philosophers, and theologians is centering on the effects of three synthetic substances—mescaline, lysergic acid, and psilocybin. What are these substances? Medicines or drugs or sacramental foods? It is easier to say what they are not. They are not narcotics, nor intoxicants, nor energizers, nor anaesthetics, nor tranquilizers. They are, rather, biochemical keys which unlock experiences shatteringly new to most Westerners. For the last two years, staff members of the Center for Research in Personality at Harvard University have engaged in systematic experiments with these substances. Our first inquiry into the biochemical expansion of consciousness has been a study of the reactions of Americans in a supportive, comfortable naturalistic setting. We have had the opportunity of participating in over one thousand individual administrations. From our observations, from interviews and reports, from analysis of questionnaire data, and from pre-and post experimental differences in personality test results, certain conclusions have emerged.

(1) These substances do alter consciousness. There is no dispute on this score.

(2) It is meaningless to talk more specifically about the "effect of the drug." Set and setting, expectation, and atmosphere account for all specificity of reaction. There is no "drug reaction" but always setting-plus-drug.

(3) In talking about potentialities it is useful to consider not just the setting-plus-drug but rather the potentialities of the human cortex to create images and experiences far beyond the narrow limitations of words and concepts. Those of us on this research project spend a good share of our working hours listening to people talk about the effect and use of consciousness-altering drugs. If we substitute the words human cortex for drug we can then agree with any statement made about the potentialities—for good or evil, for helping or hurting, for loving or fearing. Potentialities of the cortex, not of the drug. The drug is just an instrument.

"The last thing that an institution of education wants to allow you to do is to expand your consciousness . I also would like to suggest that the our educational process is an especially dangerous narcotic because it probably does direct physiological damage to your nervous system."

The Individual in the College Community an address by Timothy Leary at The Second Annual Symposium on American Values, Central State College, Ellensburg, Washington, 24-27 April 1963

***

The controversy surrounding Leary and his research team's personal experience with psychedelic drugs was unfolding in the middle of a larger legitimacy crisis in medical science about self-experimentation. From the late 1800s to mid-1900s, scientists—psychedelic and otherwise—regularly used themselves as guinea pigs in their research. Take, for example, the research team that deliberately infected themselves with yellow fever,

202

allowing them to confirm the hypothesis that mosquitoes transmit the disease, or Jonas Salk, who tested his polio vaccine on himself and his family before giving it to human subjects in clinical trials. Self-experimentation was a respected and encouraged practice during this time, and the investigators who risked their own well-being to advance scientific knowledge were considered heroic by their colleagues and the public. This image of what historian Rebecca Herzig calls the "suffering scientist," however, became a vanishing type in the postwar era as the ideal of objectivity replaced the ethic of self-sacrifice in medical research. Scientific objectivity demands a detached and disinterested investigator, one whose own messy embodiment is filtered out by methodological safeguards like standardized instruments and blinding procedures. Science studies scholars challenge this popular conception of objectivity, arguing that subjectivity can never fully be eliminated from the scientific equation, as scientific knowledge is produced by "people with bodies, situated in time, space, culture, and society, and struggling for credibility and authority." Nonetheless, the ideal of objectivity remains an entrenched feature of medical science. Self-experimentation, in which scientific knowledge emerges from investigators' subjective experiences, is incompatible with this ideal. Consequently, the credibility of self--experimentation fizzled out in medical and scientific circles in the mid--twentieth century.

Self-experimentation was an important feature of the first wave's expertise culture. Psychedelic researchers argued that direct experience with consciousness-altering substances was scientifically valuable and professionally ethical. By the early 1960s, however, their drug experiences became the subject of lively debate. A sizable number of medical professionals dismissed the results coming out of psychedelic therapy research on the grounds that researchers' personal familiarity with psychedelic drugs corrupted their objectivity. Today's researchers still grapple with this legitimacy crisis as they navigate the tenuous boundary between subjectivity (e.g., having direct experience with psychedelic drugs) and objectivity (e.g., making dispassionate claims about psychedelic drugs). On the one hand, they feel compelled to engage in a sober performance of objectivity to avoid the accusations of bias that were hurled at Leary and other early researchers. On the other hand, they agree with Leary and his contemporaries that firsthand experience with these substances is an essential skill for psychedelic researchers.

Danielle Giffort, Acid Revival, The Psychedelic Renaissance and the Quest for Medical Legitimacy, 2020

"Leary was a lax researcher who put little effort into gathering precise data."

Brendan A. Maher, the Emeritus Edward C Henderson Professor of the Psychology of Personality in the Department of Psychology - upon the death of Timothy Leary.

The Experiments Hit the News

"The Meeting"

March 15, 1962

The Harvard Crimson

The University Daily Est. 1873

By ROBERT E. SMITH

March 15, 1962

Members of the Center for Research in Personality clashed yesterday in a dramatic meeting over the right of two colleagues to continue studies on the effects of psilocybin, a consciousness-expanding drug, on graduate student subjects.

Opponents of the studies claimed that the project was run nonchalantly and irresponsibly and that alleged permanent injury to participants had been ignored or underestimated.

Crimson

I 15, 1962   March 15, 1962   PRICE TEN CENTS

Psychologists Disagree On Psilocybin Research

By ROBERT E. SMITH

Members of the Center for Research in Personality clashed yesterday in a dramatic meeting over the right of two colleagues to continue studies on the effects of psilocybin, a consciousness-expanding drug, on graduate student subjects.

Opponents of the studies claimed that the project was run nonchalantly and irresponsibly and that alleged permanent injury to participants had been ignored or underestimated.

Richard Alpert, assistant professor of Clinical Psychology, and Timothy Leary, lecturer on Clinical Psychology defended their work, saying that subjects can not be told specifically what the drug will do to them during its four-hour spell because the experimenters would then be "imposing effects and directing the experience." Alpert also asserted that the Food and Drug Administration, the University Health

Richard Alpert, assistant professor of Clinical Psychology, and Timothy Leary, lecturer on Clinical Psychology defended their work, saying that subjects can not be told specifically what the drug will do to them during its four-hour spell because the experimenters would then be "imposing effects and directing the experience." Alpert also asserted that the Food and Drug Administration, the University Health Services, and the synthesizer of psilocybin have approved the experiments.

David C. McClelland, head of the Center, said that he was concerned about the possible permanent effects of the drug but was convinced that the drug research work had been misrepresented. Presiding over a 90-minute open, meeting, McClelland said that he supported Leary's and Alpert's project

206

but viewed it, like all research at the Center, with a certain amount of skepticism.

"I wish I could treat this as scholarly disagreement," said Herbert C. Kelman, lecturer on Social Psychology and leading opponent of the psilocybin research, "but this work violates the values of the academic community." He charged a "nonchalant attitude" by Leary and Alpert toward controls of the experiments, effects on the subject, and administration of the project.

"The program," argued Kelman, "has an anti-intellectual atmosphere. Its emphasis is on pure experience, not on verbalizing findings. It is an attempt to reject most of what the psychologist tries to do."

Further, he claimed, graduate students who have experienced the drug's hallucinations and enhanced mental effects have formed an "insider" sect which views non-participants as "square." He said the program had no standards, no social usefulness, and a "perfunctory manner without an interest In what it discovers."

Leary disputed a colleague's claim that scholarly articles on psilocybin say it should be taken in a hospital setting. He said it was standard procedure to hold meetings in subjects' homes at which all in attendance were under the influence of the drug. "But no staff member," Leary added, "has ever been in a situation when he couldn't handle any eventuality."

In addition, a University Health Service physician is on 24-hour call, by telephone, with full knowledge of how to treat abnormal effects of the drug, Alpert explained.

That meeting signaled the beginning of the end for Leary at Harvard, though no one had originally set out to push him or his research off campus. In fact, it was McClelland who first proposed a progress meeting, even allowing Leary to co-sponsor it. Kelman, who had suggested the idea to McClelland, had no intention of staging an ambush—he simply wanted a chance to voice his concerns directly to the students. He had envisioned a small, orderly discussion among faculty and graduate students.

But on March 14, the gathering quickly spiraled beyond what anyone had expected. The meeting room was packed, not just with students and faculty but with outside observers, including a reporter from *The Harvard Crimson*. Word spread fast, and soon, the Boston press picked up the story. What was meant to be an internal discussion turned into a media spectacle, accelerating the controversy that would ultimately force Leary out of Harvard.

The Next Day

Boston Globe

-350 Students Take Pills-

Hallucination Drug Fought at Harvard

By NOAH GORDON

An hallucination-causing drug which has been given experimentally to 350 graduate students at Harvard has become the center of controversy between University psychologists.

The drug — psilocybin — is derived fro mmushrooms found in the mountains of Mexico. According to scientific literature, it is capable of leaving some users with psychotic after-effects.

Charge Denied

Opponents of the studies say that this fast has been ignored or underestimated by the project's principal investigators, Dr. Richard Alpert, assistant professor of clinical psychology, and Dr. Timothy Leary, lecturer on clinical psychology.

Dr. Alpert denied this to The Herald yesterday. All safeguards and controls had been exerted against psychotic after-effects, he said.

Psilocybin is related to other hallucination-causing drugs like mescaline and LSD-25. Like LSD, it is produced by the Sandos Laboratory of Switzerland. It has been administered in pill form during the Harvard experiment.

According to writer Aldous Huxley, the range of reactions to such drugs can run the gamut "from Heaven to Hell."

Subjects are under the influence of the drugs "about six hours," Dr. Alpert said.

Reactions to the drug have included a wide variety of hallucinations, insights and emotional experiences, Dr. Alpert reported. "We have run 350 subjects through the project. Each has reported a different experience," he said.

209

These activities attracted the attention of the FDA and Massachusetts law-enforcement officials, who made inquiries. Harvard and the Harvard Crimson responded by warning students against taking LSD. The warnings were picked up by the mass media— and were among the first nationally circulated publicity for LSD. As the FDA and state officials continued their investigation, a scandal broke.

Shortly after the March 15th meeting, the Massachusetts Department of Public Health initiated an investigation into Leary's program. The Department had yet to determine whether psilocybin should be classified as a "harmful" drug - if it were, only medical doctors would be authorized to legally administer it and Leary would be liable to prosecution. Eventually, Leary, Alpert, the state, and the University reached a compromise. The researchers agreed that they would turn over all their supplies to University Health Services (UHS), that they would only administer the drug with a physician present, and that they would never use undergraduates in their research. Leary escaped prosecution but chafed at having yet another set of restrictions imposed on his work.

Tuning in : Timothy Leary, Harvard, and the boundaries of experimental psychology - a thesis presented by Robin M. Wasserman, 2000.

Not Everyone was Against Them

The Harvard Crimson

The University Daily Est. 1873

The Harvard Crimson

VOL. CXXXX. No. 34.   CAMBRIDGE, MASS., SATURDAY, MARCH 17, 1962   PRICE TEN CENTS

Physiological Effects of Psilocybin Not Permanent, Psychologists Claim

"We do not think there are any physiological after-effects from psilocybin," Richard Alpert, assistant professor of Clinical Psychology, and Timothy Leary, lecturer on Clinical Psychology, agreed yesterday. "But psychological changes, positive or negative depending on the individual's response to the experiment, will occur."

Psilocybin is a drug which "frees the individual from the normal limitations of his verbal mind." Normally, Leary explained, a person is confined to the limited range of conscious and sub-conscious. Under the influence of psilocybin, however, he is often able to "step outside his own life."

Alpert reported that one of his subjects was therefore able to view his life from a new perspective when psilocybin was administered. Visual and auditory hallucinations, he continued, may result if the subject expects to experience them but are not dependent on the dosage.

At a meeting last Wednesday Alpert and Leary were criticized for failing to consider permanent effects of psilocybin. "But we would have to increase the dosage 100 times," Leary stated yesterday, "to cause permanent physiological damage."

Any profound experience such as that afforded by psilocybin exerts a continuing influence on the psychological processes of an individual, Alpert noted. Whether the influence is good or bad depends primarily on the personality. Furthermore, once a person's mind enters new regions through the drug's action, he can often return to them afterwards without psilocybin.

Yesterday Elliott Perkins '23, Master of Lowell House, called the project "more suitable for the Medical School" than for the Graduate School of Arts and Sciences. "Undergraduates," he added, "shouldn't be involved in this or any other damn experiments."

ELLIOTT PERKINS '23
"Or Any Other Damn Experiments"

SATURDAY, MARCH 17, 1962

Physiological Effects of Psilocybin Not Permanent, Psychologists Claim

"We do not think there are any physiological after-effects from psilocybin," Richard Alpert, assistant professor of Clinical Psychology, and Timothy Leary, lecturer on Clinical Psychology, agreed yesterday. "But psychological changes, positive or negative depending on the individual's response to the experiment, will occur."

211

Psilocybin is a drug which "frees the individual from the normal limitations of his verbal mind." Normally, Leary explained, a person is confined to the limited range of conscious and sub-conscious. Under the influence of psilocybin, however, he is often able to "step outside his own life."

Alpert reported that one of his subjects was therefore able to view his life from a new perspective when psilocybin was administered. Visual and auditory hallucinations, he continued, may result if the subject expects to experience them but are not dependent on the dosage.

At a meeting last Wednesday Alpert and Leary were criticized for failing to consider permanent effects of psilocybin. "But we would have to increase the dosage 100 times," Leary stated yesterday, "to cause permanent physiological damage."

Any profound experience such as that afforded by psilocybin exerts a continuing influence on the psychological processes of an individual, Alpert noted. Whether the influence is good or bad depends primarily on the personality. Furthermore, once a person's mind enters new regions through the drug's action, he can often return to them afterwards without psilocybin.

Yesterday Elliott Perkins '53, Master of Lowell House, called the project "more suitable for the Medical School" than for the Graduate School of Arts and Sciences. "Undergraduates," he added, "shouldn't be involved in this or any other damn experiments."

"I had already become a controversial figure around the Boston area, because everything that I was saying made a tremendous amount of sense to students and patients, but the doctors, the psychiatrists, the social workers, the professors, the psychologists, were not so quick to accept these theories. I was asking them to give up the status and the omniscient position which they felt their training entitled them to. I asked them to turn over the authority to the patient."

Timothy Leary, High Priest

Leary writes to President of Harvard, Dr. Pusey - March 19

There are some critical administrative and political questions that have arisen in conjunction with our work. We pose these as problems even though we presently are in the process of formulating appropriate plans which will solve many of these problems.

It is apparent from the discussion above of the potential of psilocybin that even the recognition of such potential cane about in part through the maximally flexible exploratory efforts to data. We are all only too aware of how stifling to creative endeavor the too-early imposition of controls can be.

We are, however, equally aware that there is considerable anxiety in the society about the use of such substances. This anxiety is reflected in the attempts to impose more and more limiting controls. Some of these are indeed justified by the absence of long-term data but others are the product of anxiety (and, at times, vested interest). It is difficult but necessary to separate the motives for control. We must evaluate where on the continuum of control such research should be carried out.

This much seems clear to us, the safety and success of a psilocybin experience depends upon the maturity and security of the administrator. A tolerant, supportive, democratic, non-anxious experienced administrator will almost always bring about a positive experience. The control and responsibility for administration of psilocybin should be in the hands of people so qualified. Any system of responsibility which is not based on these criteria will probably result in negative experiences.

The mistrust, misunderstanding and resentment that our work has elicited is partly our fault. The time pressures involved in our exploratory studies have led to inadequate communication with the larger community about our work and our aims. But we have also sent a definite unwillingness in many people to consider new ideas and values fairly.

We are presently deliberating with many advisors as to the means of creating a supportive community setting for this type of research. If our research programs are to achieve any order of success, they will need the close and open cooperation of our subjects and a climate or community in which our subjects can speak openly about their participation. Further, we must feel to explore new methods and ideas without fear of harassment and rumor.

Historically, the University has often provided the necessary asylum to researchers involved in work which departs radically from current cultural positions. Harvard is well known for its firm position of support for academic freedom. Therefor we anticipate that if such a supportive community for our work can be developed, the climate of Harvard will be most conducive to our continued efforts.

What criteria should be utilized in assessing (1) who can carry out research with psilocybin (2) under what conditions and (3) for what purposes? We must tamper any power we might have to control the nature of research and staff with infinite wisdom. We are presently endeavoring to form an advisory panel of men who have experience in the many fields in which psilocybin might prove be useful.

214

This panel, which would of course include experienced researchers, would evaluate and oversee the increasingly numerous requests by researchers to collaborate in the work. It la our hope that such a panel would reflect sufficient breadth of interest and opinion and sufficient statue in the community to assure the maintenance of optimal freedom for creative use of psilocybin.

At present our staff which is composed of a wide variety of researchers and scholars are contributing their time and effort to this work without financial compensation. What monies we have needed for the maintenance of an administrative office and for miscellaneous matters have been privately contributed. The psilocybin has been provided without cost by the Sandoz Laboratories.

It is unlikely that the program of research of which we conceive could be carried out with aa informal and uncertain financial structure as now exists. We are, therefore, seriously considering the possibility of creating a non-profit research foundation (probably here at Harvard) which could further stabilize our endeavors and allow for more long-term planning.

Our Staff

We have been researching with psilocybin for less than a year. In the course of that brief period the research potentials that have come to light have so enthused many of the members of the community that the research team has expanded considerably — adding to its ranks deeply committed collaborators. It is giving all of us a great deal of pleasure to be part of a team dedicated to such a significant endeavor.

This paper is a product of the joint efforts of Richard Alpert, Michael Kahn, Timothy Leary, George Litwin, Ralph Metzner and Gunther Weil, and these investigators are primarily responsible for the research described here.

The CRIMSON is pleased to announce the election of Richard L. Levine '63, of Leverett House and Fall River; and Margaret von Szeliski '64, of Barnard Hall and White Plains, N.Y., to the News Board; and of George R. Lucas II '65, of Matthews Hall and Granville, Ohio, to the Photographic Board.

A Guide to Psilocybin

The recent hectic discussions of psilocybin, a drug that alters perception, have fused six separate issues. For the benefit of those who have ben confused, the following list details these questions:

Legality: psilocybin must bear the label, "may be habit-forming," according to the Pure Food and Drug Act. It is, however, not under the jurisdiction of the Federal Narcotics Agency.

Morality: many observers and critics have strong reservations on the use of drugs like psilocybin even in carefully controlled experiments.

The conduct of research: a standing University rule forbids undergraduates to participate in experiments involving drugs; this rule is not presently under discussion, nor are there current charges that its is being violated.

The role of graduate students in research: one of the major issues in the recent meeting of the staff of the Center for Research in Personality was the degree to which experiments in scientifically dubious areas such as psilocybin were a legitimate part of the training of graduate students. The converse issue was whether participation in such research might obstruct more conventional training.

The nature of research: this is the issue that has virtually split open the staff of the Center for Research in Personality. The most vociferous critics of psilocybin research believe that it is not conducted for scientific purposes, and that the experimenters are interested in experience rather than reporting their results. A major element of the defense of research contends that scientific method and reportable results are the goal of the research. But a second element of the defense claims that experience is a legitimate goal of inquiry, and that psilocybin should be used in order to heighten perception so that the experimenters may gain new insight into personality by perceiving behavior more clearly while under influence of the drugs.

These are the issues:

After there were calls for the state to get involved President Nathan Pusey was quoted in the Crimson

Pusey Plans No Investigation of Drug

President Pusey said yesterday that the University is not planning its own investigation into the use of psilocybin at the Center for Research in Personality, and that he is confident that David C. McClelland, head of the Center, will satisfy investigators from the Massachusetts Department of Public Health.

McClelland met yesterday with Alfred J. Murphy, senior food and drug inspector at the Department, to discuss the University's use of the consciousness-expanding drug in experiments involving graduate student subjects. McClelland declined to comment on the meeting.

The dispute over the drug, which must by law bear the label "may be habit-forming," broke out at a meeting of members of the Center March 15. Part of the controversy involves the question of whether the experimenter himself should be under the influence of the drug.

Two colleagues at the Massachusetts Mental Health Center say he should not. Dr. Max Rinkel told the CRIMSON that the experimenter "should definitely not be under the influence of psilocybin at the time of his experiment. If he were, he could neither control nor observe it properly."

Both Richard Alpert and Timothy Leary, working with psilocybin at the University, hold that the experimenter must be under the mild influence of the drug to follow effectively their subjects' reactions.

Agreeing with Rinkel, Alberto DiMascio, principal investigator at the Psychopharmacology Research Laboratory, emphasized that "such studies be carried out in cooperation with a trained psychiatrist, who should possess as much knowledge as possible about the drug's actions and side effects, and the methods used to alleviate or counteract them in case any emergency should arrive."

"This physician," according to DiMascio, "should be available on call and in the building in which the experiments are being carried out, since it has been shown that the drug's actions may alter both the physical and mental processes of an individual."

Pusey Plans No Investigation of Drug

President Pusey said yesterday that the University is not planning its own investigation into the use of psilocybin at the Center for Research in Personality, and that he is confident that David C. McClelland, head of the Center, will satisfy investigators from the Massachusetts Department of Public Health.

McClelland met yesterday with Alfred J. Murphy, senior food and drug inspector at the Department, to discuss the University's use of the consciousness- expanding drug in experiments involving graduate student subjects. McClelland declined to comment on the meeting.

The dispute over the drug, which must by law bear the label "may be habit-forming." broke out at a meeting of members of the Center March 15. Part of the controversy involves the Question of whether tho experimenter himself should be under the Influence of the drug.

Two colleagues at the Massachusetts Mental Health Center say he should not. Dr. Max Rinkel told the Crimson that the experimenter "should definitely not be under the influence of psilocybin at the time of his experiment. If he were, he, could neither control nor observe II < properly."

Both Richard Alport and Timothy Leary, working with psilocybin at the University, hold that the experimenter must be under the mild influence of the drug to follow effectively their subjects' reactions.

Agreeing with Rinkel, Alborto DIMasclo, principal Investigator at the Psychopharmacology Research Laboratory, emphasized that "such studies be carried. out in cooperation with a trained psychiatrist, who should possess 0f much knowledge as possible about the drug's actions and side effects, and the methods used to alleviate or counteract them in case any emergency should arrive."

"This physician," according to DiMascio, "should be available on call and in the building in which the experiments are being carried out, since it has been shown that the drug's actions may alter both the physical and mental processes of an individual,"

Boston Globe 'Heats' the Oven

Crimson

MARCH 28, 1962   PRICE TEN CENTS

Official Declares Psilocybin Must Be Given by Doctor

George A. Michael, Deputy Commissioner of the State Health Department, expressed his opinion yesterday that psilocybin "falls into the classification of drugs that must be administered by a physician," but Richard Alpert, assistant professor of Clinical Psychology, disagreed.

"It was my understanding," Alpert stated, "that the laws of the State of Massachusetts do not forbid the use of this drug by qualified researchers under proper conditions."

According to Michael, currently conducting an inquiry into Alpert's psilocybin research, the State "harmful drug" law requires that hypnotic or somnifacient (sleep-producing) drugs be given by physicians only. Noting that the Massachusetts law is more stringent than the corresponding federal law, the commissioner said that as far as he was concerned the federal government was not important in this case, and that it "need only provide an army and navy."

219

MESCALINE REACTION

To the Editors of the CRIMSON:

An article in Tuesday's CRIMSON reviewed Huxley's theories on mescaline and related them to psilocybin studies being executed by some staff members at the Center for Research in Personality. The CRIMSON essay was a gallant attempt to summarize a most difficult subject matter, but some clarification seems needed.

1. Escape vs. Insight.

In the Doors to Perception, Aldous Huxley is concerned with the social applications of the so-called Budda drugs (mescaline, psilocybin, LSD). He refers to society's need for escapes. The escape motif should not be emphasized. For most subjects the opposite seems true. Confrontation, intense (and often painful) contact with reality more accurately characterize the experience.

2. The Center for Research in Personality is a component of the Social Relations Department. Its central function is the training of graduate students in Clinical Psychology and Personality. Research by staff members is a second important goal of the Center. Several staff members and graduate students at the Center for Research in Personality are engaged in the development of methods for behavior change. The efficacy of psilocybin in behavior change is one of several techniques being studied.

3. The "investigators of psilocybin" are not "unbounded in their enthusiasm." Unbounded concern would be a more accurate diagnosis—concern for the many problems created by the consciousness-expanding drugs. Problems

of conceptualization. Problems of measurement. Problems of application and follow-up. Problems of interpretation. Problems of control.

Our first research study addressed itself to the range of reactions of subjects taking psilocybin in a naturalistic setting. A wide range of subjects were part of this study—professors, poets, priests, prisoners, "problem-cases." Our conclusions—set and setting, expectation and emotional atmosphere (in particular the fears and intentions of the experimenter) account for almost all of the specificity of reaction.

For the past six months we have centered on systematic and controlled studies of the effects of psilocybin in prisoner rehabilitation, in individual counseling, and in experimental situations.

Like all research studies executed by University personnel we have followed the codes governing use of subjects. No secrecy. Careful preparatory orientation. Medical screening. On call medical coverage. All subjects are informed volunteers. No undergraduates or minors.

Consciousness expanding drugs may some day contribute to human welfare by increasing understanding of the mind, by suggesting new methods of educational research, and behavior change. This work is just beginning. Systematic scientific studies in this field, as in any other, will produce the facts.

Richard Alpert,
Timothy Leary,
Center for Research In Personality.

The Harvard Crimson

The University Daily Newspaper—Founded 1873
Copyright 1962 The Harvard Crimson

Second class postage

"I had already become a controversial figure around the Boston area, because everything that I was saying made a tremendous amount of sense to students and patients, but the doctors, the psychiatrists, the social workers, the professors, the psychologists, were not so quick to accept these theories. I was asking them to give up the status and the omniscient position which they felt their training entitled them to. I asked them to turn over the authority to the patient."

Timothy Leary, High Priest

The Good Friday Experiment - April 1962

"I regard the experience as a personal 'shaking to the foundations.' The radical facing of myself forced - or perhaps I should say released by the drug - was a trauma the depth of which was totally unexpected. I would describe the experience as a conversion experience of the most radical nature rather than a mystical experience of the classical variety as Stace* has defined it. Yet, though without many of the indications of mystical experience, I know I will understand the mystics much better, having had the experience." - Participant

*Walter Terence Stace (1886 –1967) - From 1932 to 1955 he was employed by Princeton University in the Department of Philosophy. He is most renowned for his work in the philosophy of mysticism, and for books like *Mysticism and Philosophy* (1960) and *Teachings of the Mystics* (1960).

Marsh Chapel, Boston University, MA

The Good Friday experiment was conducted on Good Friday on April 20, 1962. In it, 20 theological students from relatively similar religious and socioeconomic backgrounds after medical and psychiatric screening were carefully prepared. Several days before the experiment, in groups of four with two leaders for each group, all 30 participants listened over loud speakers to a meditative Good Friday worship service in a private basement chapel, while the actual service was in progress in the church. Above the experiment was so designed that half of the subject received 30 milligrams of psilocybin, and the rest who became the control group got as an active placebo, 200 milligrams of nicotinic acid, which causes no psychic effects, only warmth and tingling of the skin. The drugs were administered double-blind so that neither the experimenter nor the participants knew the specific contents of any capsule data were collected by tape recordings, written account, and the Pahnke Mystical Experience questionnaire and the personal interview.

Walter Pahnke the originator of the experiment was a ministerial degree student at the Harvard Divinity as well Medical Doctor.

Dr. Pahnke wanted to do his doctoral thesis on psychedelic experience: a medically supervised, double-blind pre-and post-tested, scientifically controlled, up-to-date experiment on the production of religious ecstasy as described by Christian visionaries and measured by questionnaires, checklists, and interviews. This was just what we had been waiting for.

"How many subjects, Pahnke?" I asked.

"Thirty in the control group and thirty in the experimental group. They'll take the drug—or a placebo—in church on Good Friday with organ music and a sermon and the whole ritual going full blast. He added with boy-scout sincerity, "I've read your comments about set and setting."

"You want to turn on thirty people at the same time in a public place?"

"Yup. In the Boston University Cathedral. I've already spoken with Dean Thurmond, and he'll let us use the small chapel."

"Pahnke, that is the most reckless suggestion I've heard in weeks. Turning on thirty inexperienced people at once. You don't understand what you are dealing with. A psychedelic experience is intimate. It's intense. You laugh at cosmic jokes. You moan in cosmic terror. You may end up on the floor wrestling with God and the devil. The first session must take place in protected, quiet, secure surroundings."

Timothy Leary - Flashbacks

When Walter Pahnke proposed a double-blind experiment designed to find out whether psilocybin could actually induce an authentic religious experience, Tim did everything he could to stand in his way. Pahnke's plan was to assemble divinity students from the Andover Newton Theological Seminary in the small downstairs chapel of Marsh Chapel on the campus of Boston University on Good Friday. Half would be given psilocybin, the other half nicotinic acid. The subjects would be divided into groups, with

227

the two guides for each group taking thirty milligrams of psilocybin. The Good Friday sermon delivered by Howard Thurmond, the black minister who was Martin Luther King's mentor, would then be piped into the chapel. Neither subjects, nor guides, nor experimenters would know who had taken what. Sounding like a smalltown Irish parish priest, Tim later wrote, "I really had to laugh at this caricature of the experimental design applied to that most sacred experience. If he had proposed giving aphrodisiacs to twenty virgins to produce a mass orgasm, it wouldn't have sounded further out." As a medical doctor, Pahnke tried to reassure Tim by telling him he could legally administer any drug he liked. He could also inject those having a bad experience with tranquilizers to bring them down. Tim responded by telling Pahnke he should first take the drug several times himself so he would be familiar with it. Pahnke refused. For his study to be accepted as unbiased and objective, he needed to preserve his "psychedelic virginity."

Good Friday - Greenfield

The following if from *Being Ram Dass*

As scientists, Tim and I didn't have the tools to really explain this (mystical experience). We didn't know of any published research that tracked with our experiences. Since we'd had a few religious thinkers already participate in our research, like Huston Smith and Alan Watts, we turned to them to help us explore this mystical quality. Tim also made several visits to the Harvard Divinity School to enlist faculty and students who might want to try psychedelics. Smith began hosting a Sunday gathering at his house for us to run sessions. People who stopped by included Walter Houston Clark, a professor of psychology of religion at Newton Theological School, and Walter Pahnke, a medical doctor who was pursuing a PhD at Harvard in philosophy and religion.

228

During a gathering at Huston Smith's house, Walter Pahnke, proposed an idea for his thesis dissertation. He wanted to create a careful study in experimental mysticism to establish whether psychedelics could induce a genuine religious experience. He proposed giving a group of divinity students psilocybin during a church service on Good Friday. Tim and I helped Pahnke maximize every factor of the set and setting to produce a religious experience. Thanks to Walter Houston Clark, we found twenty volunteer subjects at Newton Theological School, whom we pretested and screened with psychiatric interviews. Huston Smith was among the volunteers. Half the group would receive psilocybin, while a control group received a placebo. There would be trained graduate-student guides to work with the students, and afterward,

Pahnke would chart participants' reactions based in part on the work of the Princeton-based philosopher W. T. Stace.

If what our Harvard colleagues wanted was systematic research with controls, this was it, the gold standard, a double-blind, medically supervised experiment. The only problem was that our psilocybin was under tight control, and Farnsworth and a newly formed supervisory committee were dragging their feet on approving the study. Tim tracked down the psilocybin we needed by contacting a psychiatrist in Worcester.

On April 20, 1962, we convened at Boston University's Marsh Chapel. No one could predict what would happen, so we agreed to isolate the participants in the basement. Half the group received an envelope with a pill of psilocybin; the other half received an envelope with a pill of nicotinic acid, which mimicked the onset of a psychedelic trip by producing a mild niacin flush. The inspiring sermon by the chapel's charismatic preacher, Dean Howard Thurman, was piped into the basement from above. As hymns began to play, the students settled in on the base¬ment's benches. None of them were told what to expect.

Neither the students nor the observers knew who got the psychedelic and who got the placebo, but it was soon obvious. The nicotinic acid wore off, and students who had taken it sat listening attentively, whereas those on psilocybin lay down or wandered around the room, fixated on their visions. The psilocybin subjects, it turned out, experienced states and levels of consciousness that were indistinguishable from classic mystical experiences. The control group by and large did not.

As far as we were concerned, the experiment was a complete success. It laid to rest doubts about psychedelics as a vehicle for mystical insight. Although for us it was one experiment among many, it quickly became famous in psychological and religious circles.

Walter N. Pahnke

©*The International Journal of Parapsychology, Vol. VIII, No. 2, Spring 1966, pp. 295-313.*

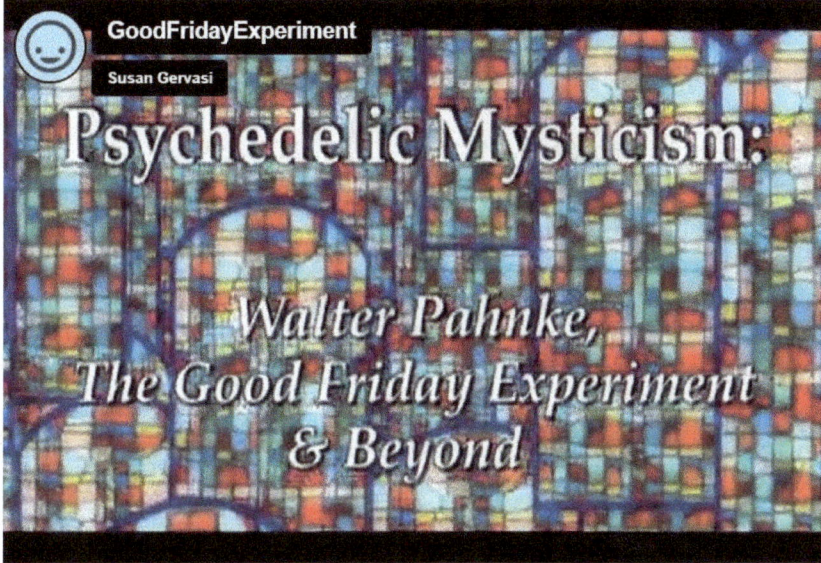

https://www.youtube.com/watch?v=WEsWmpf6dgc

Time to Get Out of Town

November 1962

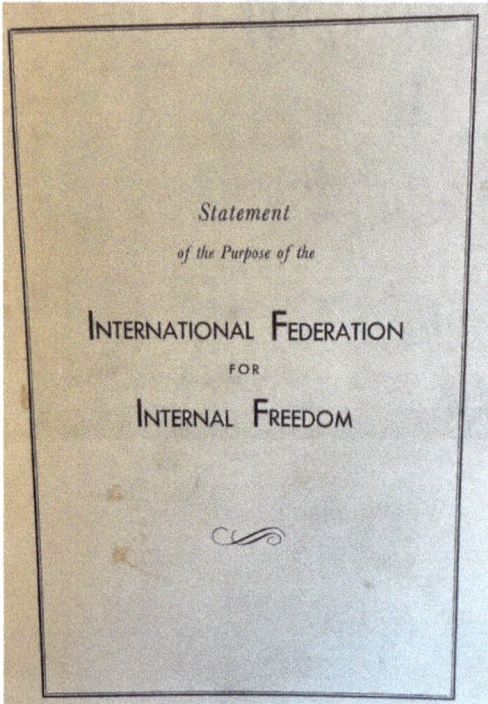

In November 1962, Leary, Alpert, and 9 other academics formed the *International Federation for Internal Freedom*. The group's stated purpose was to encourage people to form research groups to explore consciousness and promote psychedelics research. But the implicit purpose was the democratization of psychedelics—the idea that everyone should be given the opportunity to expand their consciousness using the drugs.

New York Times, December 14, 1962

HARVARD DEBATES MIND-DRUG 'PERIL'

Psychologists Say Dean Errs on 'Danger' of Stimulants

By FRED M. HECHINGER

Special to The New York Times.

NEW YORK.

Two Harvard psychologists charged that statements made by the dean, in an effort to stop the use of such drugs among undergraduates, were "reckless and inaccurate" from the scientific point of view.

They added that action impeding experimentation at Harvard, other leading universities, medical schools and governmental health agencies had led to a "scientific underground in the United States" to evade social pressures and legal barriers.

Dr. Richard Alpert, assistant professor of clinical psychology and education and associate director of the Laboratory of Human Development, and Dr. Timothy Leary, lecturer on clinical psychology, fired back at recent warnings by Dean Monro that "intellectual promotion"

HARVARD DEBATES MIND-DRUG 'PERIL'

Psychologists Say Dean Errs on 'Danger' of Stimulants

By FRED M. HECHINGJER Special to The New York Times.

Two Harvard psychologists charged that statements made by the dean, in an effort to stop the use of such drugs among undergraduates, were "reckless and inaccurate" from the scientific point of view.

They added that action impeding experimentation at Harvard, other leading universities, medical schools and governmental health agencies had led to a "scientific underground in the United States" to evade social pressures and legal barriers.

Dr. Richard Alpert, assistant professor of clinical psychology and education and associate director of the Laboratory of Human Development, and Dr. 'Timothy Leary, lecturer on clinical psychology, fired back at recent warnings by Dean Monro that "intellectual promotion" of the "consciousness-expand- drugs constituted a serious hazard among students. The dean termed the drugs "mind distorting."

Most prominent among these drugs is psilocybin. Others are known as mescaline and LSD.

Dean Monro acted with the full support of Dr. Dana L. Farnsworth, director of the Harvard's health services and a noted medical authority. The dean said there was "unanimity among our doctors that these drugs are dangerous" and might lead to serious mental illness.

These statements were challenged by the two psychologists in a letter to The Harvard Crimson which 'also had published the earlier warnings. They said that the "hysteria" about the effects of "consciousness-expanding" drugs constituted a danger to scientific research.

234

Effect Held to Be Mild

While conceding that Dean Monro had an administrative responsibility "to pacify worries about undergraduates' activity," the psychologists charged that he was "ill-formed[1] about the effects of these drugs."

Dr.'s Alpert and Leary described the changes produced in the mind by the "consciousnessexpanding" drug as similar to those produced in the mind by the printed word or by the power of suggestion. They said that there was "no factual evidence that 'consciousness-expanding' drugs are uniquely dangerous and considerable evidence that they are safe and beneficial."

They said in their letter to the student newspaper that "there is no reason to believe that consciousness-experiences are any more dangerous than psychoanalysis or a four-year enrollment in Harvard College."

The psychologists charged that "if you try to apply these potentials within the conventional institutional format you are side-tracked, silenced, blocked or fired." They said that "competent and recognized scientists" were being barred from such research "not only at Harvard but in the top universities and medical schools in the country and in the United States Institute of Public Health."

This they added, had "for the first time in American history" led to "a scientific underground."

Last year, the Massachusetts Public Health Department ruled that psilocybin is to be administered only in the presence of a medical doctor.

And the News Kept Coming

The Harvard Crimson

The University Daily Est. 1873

On Monday December 10, 1962 Timothy Leary and Richard Alpert sat down to write a scathing rebuke in the "Letters to the Editor" section of the Harvard Crimson. Leary's attempts at research into psychedelics, psilocybin and LSD specifically, had come under fire from the administration of the school. Leary and Alpert were angered at the use of inflammatory language that the dean had recently used in a warning he had issued to the students at Harvard. Leary and Alpert claimed that if you want to test the "potentials [of psychedelic drugs] within the conventional institutional format you are sidetracked, silenced, blocked, or fired."

On December 9th 1962 the Harvard Crimson foreshadowing the maelstrom of anti-psychedelic articles in national print media, an article was published that asserted Leary and Alpert were being investigated by the FBI and the FDA.

The United States' Print Media and its War on Psychedelic Research in the 1960s - Jessica Bracco

The Harvard Crimson

The University Daily Est. 1873

Leary and Alpert Attack Monro Stand On Drugs Offer Defense of Research in Psilocybin, Call University's Position 'Ill-Informed' NO WRITER ATTRIBUTED December 11,1962

In a statement issued last night in response to questions asked by the CRIMSON, Timothy Leary discounted reports of widespread undergraduate use of psilocybin and similar drugs. "Unfounded rumors about consciousness-expanding drugs have been at fever pitch for the last two years. . .Locally and nationally there seems to be intense interest in consciousness expansion, but little access to the drugs"

However, Leary and Alpert did not join Dean Monro in warning undergraduates to steer clear of the drugs. When asked whether he thought Monro's warning was out of place, Leary stated: "We understand Dean Monro's desire to pacify worries about undergraduate activity, but we believe he is ill-informed about the effects of these drugs".

The Harvard Crimson

The University Daily Est. 1873

Psilocybin Expert Raps Leary, Alpert on Drugs

By Efrem Sigel

December 12, 1962

An expert on psilocybin and other "consciousness expanding" drugs (LSD, mescaline) yesterday criticized Timothy Leary and Richard Alpert for raising a "false issue of scientific or academic freedom" in their charges that research on these drugs is being blocked at Harvard and other universities. Read article >>>

The Harvard Crimson

The University Daily Est. 1873

December 13, 1962

(Following is the full text of the letter submitted to the CRIMSON Monday by Timothy Leary and Richard Alpert.)

To the Editors of the CRIMSON:

In three recent CRIMSON articles (widely reprinted in the national press) Harvard administrators have stated, that consciousness-expanding drugs (LSD, mescaline, psilocybin) are "a serious hazard to the mental health and stability even of apparently normal people." While these statements are conservative from the administrative point of view, they are reckless and inaccurate from the scientific. The published facts and the philosophical-political implications deserve thoughtful review. To understand the importance of this issue, it is necessary to realize that more is involved than the more handlings of drugs. What is in question is the freedom or control of consciousness, the limiting or expanding of man's awareness. Let us consider some of the facts.

These drugs are powerful nonverbal mind-altering substances--probably the most powerful ever known to man. Now any stimulus, verbal or nonverbal, which presents itself to the nervous system changes the bio-chemistry of your nervous system. If you want to play the labelling game you can call some of these changes dangerous and others beneficial. You can label some artificial and others natural. Compare this to the written word. Can the written word be dangerous? Is the written word natural? Are nonverbal stimuli such as the sacred mushroom of Mexico artificial? Is the chemical essence of the mushroom dangerous?

238

Harvard Archives Restrictions on Further Research

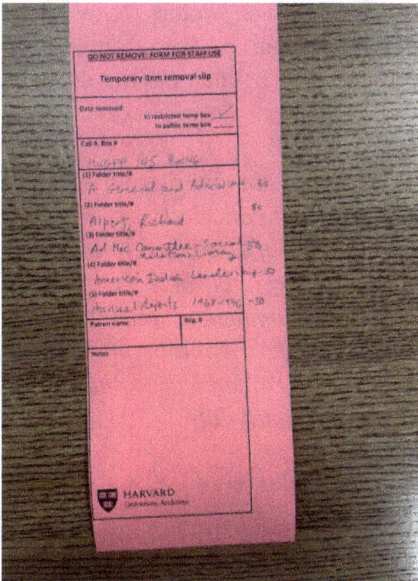

During my research in the Harvard Archives, I encountered a number of pink slips in various folders indicating restrictions on the materials I was seeking. One such slip was in a folder belonging to Richard Alpert—restricted for 80 years! I was stunned that materials associated with Dr. Alpert (Ram Dass) could be considered so "secret," especially given his remarkable openness across hundreds of lectures and public appearances over the decades as a cultural icon of the psychedelic movement.

When I inquired about possible exceptions that might grant me access to this folder, I contacted the head archivist.

In researching Hollis, I found and could access materials that were helpful to my research, except for one item that fell under the 'R80' restriction. The item which I requested on March 2, 2023, was:

Records of the Dean of Harvard College, 1889-1995. General Subject Files of Dean Monro. "Drugs 1962-August 1964," 2 folders [UAIII 5.33, Box 488] R-80. They consist of material related to the dismissal of Timothy Leary and Richard Alpert and the use of hallucinogenic drugs in scientific research by Harvard students.

On the following day, March 3, 2023, I received an email from Harvard Archives telling me, *"This request has been canceled as Harvard University regulations close any official records of the University for 50 years and close any documents containing personal and confidential information (grades, evaluations, professional recommendations etc.) for a minimum of 80-years. The records in these folders contain information about Harvard students and faculty that make them subject to the "R80" year rule. These materials are closed to research until July 1, 2045."*

I want to appeal this decision based on a 1989 vote of the Harvard Corporation, which **allows** *"The Director of the University Library, or his/her representative, usually the Curator of the University Archives, **to authorize the use of University records** more than fifty years old (or records concerning individuals which shall be more than eighty years old, or the individual being alive, after his/her decease, whichever is later),* *provided they are not fragile original records that might be damaged by use, in which cases copies will be provided."*

My inquiry eventually reached the desk of the Dean of Harvard College, Rakesh Khurana, who curtly denied the request without providing a reason.

In the meantime I found cases in the past where exceptions had been made where acess was given for these types of restrictions. This gave me some evidence to pursue this request further which eventually lead me to the President of Harvard College. After exchanging emails with his office and

The End

ADMINISTRATION

The President of Harvard University is vulnerable to criticism on all sides. He is at once the head of the most impressive array of academicians in America and the director of a $40 million a year business. As the primary policy maker for both educational and financial questions, he makes far-reaching decisions which cannot but polarize the Harvard community. NATHAN MARSH PUSEY '28, President of Harvard University, was strongly attacked by the Harvard *Crimson* for his failure to appoint a new Dean of the Faculty of Arts and Sciences to replace McGeorge Bundy. His eventual selection of Franklin Ford was widely hailed.

President Pusey sees Harvard's position as one of leadership in a universal academic community. Soon after assuming his position in 1953, he set about making expansion plans to help the University fulfill its obligations. The Program for Harvard College, which met its goal of $82.5 million early in 1960, has gone far in financing the strengthening of liberal education at Harvard. Faculty salaries have been raised dramatically and some twenty new academic chairs have been endowed. New physical facilities such as the Loeb Drama Center, the Center for the Visual Arts and the Leverett Towers have sprung up all over the campus. Programs in International Legal Studies, Middle Eastern Studies and East Asian Studies have been established and provided with superb facilities. In the year that the Program succeeded, a $58 million Program for Harvard Medicine was begun.

Tensions between Harvard University Alpert and Leary, reached a breaking point. The university administration, led by the dean of the faculty and the dean of the college, had decided that Alpert and Leary's unconventional methods and research practices had become intolerable. Armed with a list of allegations and sources of information, the deans launched an investigation into the two psychologists' activities. Their goal was clear: uncover evidence of wrongdoing, particularly regarding their controversial use of psilocybin, a psychoactive substance, in their research.

The investigation began with a series of interviews. The deans summoned many undergraduates and others who had been involved with Alpert and Leary's work, assuring each individual that no action would be taken against them. They were only interested in gathering facts about Alpert and Leary's conduct. However, to the Deans' frustration, nearly all of the students and participants refused to cooperate. In fact, most of them expressed unwavering loyalty to the two psychologists, standing by them despite the deans' efforts to extract damaging information.

242

There was, however, one exception. A senior student, who believed others had already spoken to the investigators, decided to break his silence. He informed the Deans that Richard Alpert had given him psilocybin during a personal session in 1962, a revelation that contradicted university policies prohibiting the use of undergraduates in such experiments. This was exactly the evidence the university needed to proceed with disciplinary action.

On Tuesday, May 14, 1963, Harvard President Nathan Pusey summoned Alpert to his office. In this tense meeting, Pusey formally charged Alpert with violating the university's prohibition by giving psilocybin to an undergraduate. Worse yet, Alpert had allegedly assured university officials that he had not given the drug to any undergraduate after the prohibition went into effect. This breach of trust, combined with the violation of research ethics, was a critical turning point in the case against Alpert and marked the beginning of the end for his time at Harvard.

This incident, which eventually led to Alpert's dismissal from the university, highlighted the growing divide between traditional academic structures and the radical, experimental approaches being explored by Alpert and Leary. Their work with psychedelic substances, though groundbreaking, ultimately clashed with the institution's policies and norms, setting the stage for their departure from the academic world and their continued exploration of human consciousness outside the bounds of Harvard.

The Dismissals

Harvard Fires 2 in Drug Row

By HERBERT BLACK

Two Harvard psychologists who for months have been the center of controversy over experiments with hallucinatory drugs, with some of the tests involving Harvard students, have been dropped by the university.

They are Richard Alpert, professor of clinical psychology, and Timothy F. Leary, lecturer on clinical psychology.

Alpert's parting with Harvard is an out-and-out dismissal, the first under the regime of Pres. Nathan M. Pusey.

The reason for his dismissal, according to Dr. Pusey, is that Alpert violated a promise not to give consciousness-expanding drugs to Harvard students without permission of the university and prior clearance by the college medical department.

Leary, on the other hand, has been "relieved" of his post for "failure to keep classroom appointments." The Corporation voted to relieve him of his pay as of Apr. 30. He went to California without notifying officials and shipped

DROPPED by Harvard. Richard Alpert, clinical psychology professor (left), and Timothy F. Leary, lecturer on same subject.

245

ALPERT'S LETTER TO PUSEY

An Open Letter

NO WRITER ATTRIBUTED
May 29, 1963

Dear President Pusey,

(The letter below was given to the CRIMSON the evening of May 27, 1963, by Richard Alpert, whose appointment in Harvard University was terminated yesterday.) May 15, 1963

At our meeting last Tuesday, you advised me that you would bring the matter of the termination of my contract before the Corporation at its next meeting. This issue is not entirely separable from the views of the University toward our research in general. Therefore, I am taking this opportunity to bring to the attention of you and the members of the Corporation some of the cogent matters associated with our work. By this means, I hope to prevent the broader issues from being totally submerged beneath the myriad lesser decisions (e.g., my contract) which have to date constituted Harvard's official "position" and expressed concern.

We have carried out our studies of psychedelic (mind-manifesting) materials at the University from the autumn of 1960 until the end of 1962, when the association of our research with Harvard was formally terminated. Consequently we organized I.F.I.F., through which we have continued our research activities. During the period when the research was affiliated with Harvard, we worked safely with over four hundred subjects in a series of studies at the Concord Reformatory, within the local religious community, and at the University. These studies explored the effects of altering states of consciousness on (1) the creative process, (2) the religious experience, (3) the rate of learning, (4) behavior change, (5) aesthetic experience, (6) interpersonal relations, and (7) flexibility of thought process. Some of our efforts have been directed toward the development of adequate models for conceptualization of these profound mind-manifesting experiences (very much in the tradition of William James). Our preliminary research, as well as studies pursued by others in the field, indicates that psychedelics are among the most powerful consciousness-altering substances known to man and certainly deserve our most serious and creative attention.

As you know, any research which has the potentiality of affecting the institutions of a culture does not long go unnoticed. Our research was debated by our colleagues, and investigated by both the state and federal governments in the spring of 1961. It was also the subject of controversial discussion at a leading international psychological convention in Copenhagen, where it received support from men such as Professor Henry Murray and Aldous Huxley.

Publicly, this research produced one of the major issues for news and editorial comment in the local press and has now come to the attention of the country's mass media (cf. Life, March 15, 1963; Time, March 29, 1963; the TV forum "Open End"--to be shown in the Boston area Sunday, May 26). It will continue to receive increasing attention in the months to come.

There are many indications to suggest that explorations with psychedelic materials promise to be among the most important and dramatic fields of investigation of the next decade. Research of the "inner space" of man's consciousness in the future may well parallel the explorations of the external world now under way.

Harvard University has been long considered a fearless leader in providing a climate of encouragement and support for historically significant exploration and discovery. We propose that research designed to study the

247

use of psychedelic substances for man's growth and education is just such exploration. We urge you and the policy-making bodies of the University to review from both an immediate and historical perspective the public position into which Harvard has cast itself with regard to this research.

My main concern is not with the disposition of my contract, nor with the threats to my colleagues who have been involved with us in this research. As our work continues and comes increasingly to the public's attention, we shall all be in a better position to determine how wisely all of us have acted in the specifics of this controversy. Of much greater import is the stand taken by a leading university toward this new exploring of man's consciousness.

I am taking the liberty of sending copies of this letter, as well as the statement of purpose of I.F.I.F. to the members of the Corporation. To you and to the members, I wish both vision and wisdom in your deliberations.

OUSTED EDUCATOR REBUTS HARVARD

Denies He Broke Pledge in Testing Drugs on Students

By JOHN H. FENTON
Special to The New York Times

CAMBRIDGE, Mass., May 28 —Dr. Richard Alpert denied today that he had broken faith with Harvard University by involving an undergraduate in a psychological test using hallucinogenic drugs.

Dr. Alpert, an assistant professor of psychology and of education, has been dismissed, according to an announcement yesterday by Dr. Nathan M. Pusey, Harvard's president, to The Harvard Crimson, the undergraduate daily newspaper.

At an impromptu news conference today, Dr. Alpert said the reason for his discharge was "open to a variety of in-

OUSTED EDUCATOR REBUTS HARVARD

Denies He Broke Pledge in Testing Drugs on Students

By John H. Fenton

Special to The New York Times

CAMBRIDGE, Mass., May 28, 1963 - Dr. Richard Alpert denied today that he had broken faith with Harvard University by involving an undergraduate in a psychological test using hallucinogenic drugs. Dr. Alpert, an assistant professor of psychology and of education, has been dismissed, according to an announcement yesterday by Dr. Nathan M. Pusey, Harvard's president, to The Harvard Crimson, the undergraduate daily newspaper.

At an impromptu news conference today, Dr. Alpert said the reason for his discharge was "open to a variety of interpretations." Harvard, he declared, "has chosen one which technically justifies their action and which effectively closes off our association with them."

Dr. Alpert said he used psilocybin on one undergraduate a year ago. He said he and Dr. Leary had turned down 200 requests from undergraduates to participate in the research.

"My statement to Dean [John B.] Monro reassuring him that our interest was not in pursuing research among undergraduates," said Dr. Alpert. "I do not feel that this single exception constitutes bad faith on our part." the university had allowed the experiments on the condition that no undergraduate would be used to test the drugs without clearance from a staff member of the university medical services.

In his statement to The Crimson, Dr. Pusey said Dr. Alpert had assured Dean Monro that he had not given drugs to any undergraduate. In a letter to

Dr. Pusey, written since the Harvard Corporation voted his dismissal on May 20, Dr. Alpert said he and his associates had worked "safely" on more than 400 subjects, in prisons, among religious community members in Cambridge and among graduate students at the university.

Dr. Alpert said he used psilocybin on one undergraduate a year ago. He said he and Dr. Leary had turned down 200 requests from undergraduates to participate in the research.

"My statement to Dean [John B.] Monro reassuring him that our interest was not in pursuing research among undergraduates," said Dr. Alpert. "I do not feel that this single exception constitutes bad faith on our part." the university had allowed the experiments on the condition that no undergraduate would be used to test the drugs without clearance from a staff member of the university medical services.

In his statement to The Crimson, Dr. Pusey said Dr. Alpert had assured Dean Monro that he had not given drugs to any undergraduate. In a letter to Dr. Pusey, written since the Harvard Corporation voted his dismissal on May 20, Dr. Alpert said he and his associates had worked "safely" on more than 400 subjects, in prisons, among religious community members in Cambridge and among graduate students at the university.

Side Notes

The dismissal of Leary and Alpert marked the first time a Harvard professor had been fired in over a hundred years. Nathan Pusey, the president of Harvard, personally conducted a closed-door investigation that included the interrogation of various undergraduate students who allegedly had taken psychedelic drugs with Leary and Alpert.

Pusey's investigation yielded only one confession. Ronnie Winston, a male undergraduate, admitted to taking psilocybin pills with Professor Alpert during the spring semester of 1962. Winston, heir to the Harry Winston

251

jewelry fortune, famously remarked to the President of Harvard: "It was the most profound experience of any of the courses that I have had here [at Harvard]" (Dass and Metzner 90).

RONALD HARIVMAN WINSTON
Born: January 10, 1941, in New York, N. Y. Prepared at Riverdale H.S., Riverdale, N. Y. Home Address: 927 Fifth Ave., New York, N. Y. Field of Concentration: English. MIT Rocket Research Society; Jubilee Committee; Hasty Pudding; Signet; D. U. Club. American Rocket Society National Award.

Pusey's investigation also uncovered a clandestine affair between Alpert and Winston. In public accounts of the scandal, Harvard authorities carefully suppressed all references to the homosexual affair and fired Alpert for giving psilocybin to "one undergraduate."

President Pusey's press release on May 27, 1963, states that " . . . Dr. Alpert violated an agreement which he had entered into in November 1961, not to involve undergraduates.

Timothy Leary - The Harvard Years, Introduction

Later, Alpert "confessed"

"I did break a contract," *(Alpert)* said finally. A year and a half ago I had a very close friend who was a junior at Harvard. I want to keep his name out of this. He had been having black-market-type experiences with the drugs and they had been pretty lousy. "I was spending my weekends with him. When you have something and it means something to someone you care about, but you can't give it to him, it bugs you. "I gave him a very light dose. "I had been so good. I turned down over two hundred guys. But my friend had a buddy [Andrew Weil] who got very irate and went to the authorities. "Some day it will be quite humorous that a professor was fired for supplying a student with the most profound educational experience in my life.' That's what he told the Dean it was."

Timothy Leary - The Harvard Years, James Penner

'Harvard Psychedelic Club,'

an explosion that shaped Andrew Weil, Huston Smith & Ram Dass

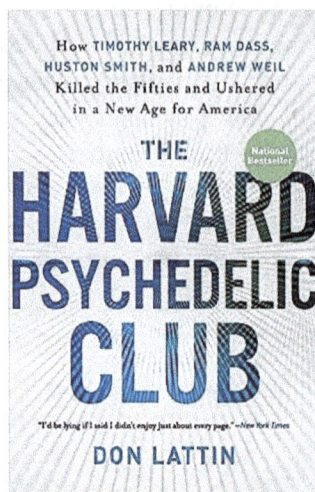

(**DON** Lattin and **DAVID** Crumm)

DON: But, at Harvard, this all quickly became a cult around Leary and Alpert.

DAVID: That brings us to Richard Alpert, better known as Ram Dass—the "Be Here Now" guy for millions of Baby Boomers and still a major figure in   American   spirituality.

Back at Harvard, well, I have to say it—he comes across in your book as a pretty ambitious young jerk, too. In a way, Alpert and Weil sort of vie for the "bad guy" role in this drama that finally burst out into Page 1 headlines across American news media. Maybe it wasn't entirely Alpert's fault. He was still trying to come to terms with his complicated sexual orientation.

He hadn't yet gone off to India, where he went through this spiritual transformation into what we know today as Ram Dass.

At the time, he was a very ambitious young academic, right?

DON: Yeah, he was young and very ambitious. He was a career-climbing academic at Harvard who didn't have tenure yet but was definitely on tenure track. He was very popular at Harvard—known as a terrific lecturer and a very charming guy. Like the Buddhist scholar Alan Watts, Alpert has always had this talent for explaining esoteric ideas from Eastern mysticism to a Western audience.

Back at Harvard, though, Alpert wasn't known as an especially brilliant scholar. A very popular teacher, yes—but he had a lot of things going on in his life. He was struggling with his sexual addictions, among other things at   that   time.

I spent three days interviewing him on Maui, where he now lives. (*That's him, now, at left.*) He really did have breakthrough experiences with psychedelics that helped him to accept his homosexuality, which at the time was very difficult for him to do.

He also had all these attachments to materialism. He owned a sports car and an airplane, too! He had filled his apartment with antiques. By all appearances, he had made it. Here he was in his early 30s—an assistant professor at Harvard and he owned all this cool stuff.

DAVID: Then it all came crashing down.

DON: Yeah, Alpert was the one who was kicked out of Harvard for giving Psilocybin to a student—and Leary got kicked out along with him. It all was due to what happened with Andrew Weil and Weil's story in the Harvard Crimson newspaper.

DAVID: Ironically, this all turned out to be a good thing for Ram Dass, as we know him now.

DON: He wound up coming to San Francisco and he was a big part of the Haight-Ashbury scene. But he still was thinking of himself as a phony with lots of self doubts. Then, in 1967, he goes to India and spends a couple of years in this very intense training in meditation. He comes back to the U.S. bearded and robed as the beatific Baba Ram Dass, later shortened to just Ram Dass.

What's interesting is that his message to the Baby Boomers who were experimenting with drugs is that there are kinder and gentler ways to experience mysticism through meditation and other methods. He actually encouraged people to move beyond drugs and find spiritual practices to feed their lives, instead.

DAVID: So, let's talk about Dr. Andrew Weil—the angry bad boy in your drama. Hard to recognize him, considering the lovable bear of a man we know today! (*That's him in a hot tub more recently, above.*) Born in 1942, Weil always was absolutely brilliant. He winds up at Harvard as this fiercely independent whiz kid. He was interested in alternative treatments quite early. While he was still a student, he wrote a paper on the narcotic properties of nutmeg.

In your book, you talk about how desperately he wanted to get in on these Harvard drug experiments. You write that, when they refused to let him into their inner circle, there pretty clearly was "the possibility of ... malicious intent" in his use of the Harvard Crimson to "out" these guys—which exploded into front-page news coast to coast.

So, now that he's a beloved celebrity himself, what did Dr. Weil say about this book you were writing?

256

DON: He only gave me one hour for an interview. Of course, I had lots of research material about his role in all of this. Then, when I was doing interviews, I did spend the one hour with him. I expected I would hear more from him than I have, but he seems fine with what I've written.

DAVID: I keep using this word "jerk" to describe some of the confrontational behavior that unfolded at Harvard. I mean, people wound up fired from their jobs as a result of this. Harvard was embarrassed by all the media attention. There was a lot of angry behavior going on back then.

DON: Andrew Weil was a brilliant young kid. He was so smart that, when he started at Harvard in 1960, he actually started as a sophomore. He had read Huxley's "Doors of Perception." He worked on an undergraduate thesis at Harvard on nutmeg as a psychotropic substance.

He was very interested in these things Leary and Alpert were pursuing. These guys were the talk of the town. He'd heard that grad students were taking drugs and having these incredible experiences. Weil and his friend Ronnie Winston went to Leary's office and volunteered to become a part of this project. He and Ronnie wanted to become research subjects.

Leary asked if they were grad students—if they were old enough to do this. They weren't old enough and he didn't let them participate.

But, Weil was very ambitious and a little surreptitious and he got some Harvard stationery and obtained his own supply of drugs—and they wound up doing their own little undergraduate research project. Then, soon after that, Ronnie Winston runs into Richard Alpert at a party and they strike up a friendship. Alpert leads Ronnie in some self-exploratory Psilocybin experiences. Ram Dass today says he had some romantic interest in Ronnie, but both of them—Ram Dass and Ronnie—say there was no sexual relationship.

257

But Andrew Weil heard about this and he was jealous that Ronnie was getting in on the drug experiments with these guys. He was upset. He decided to bring down Leary and Alpert partly out of jealousy and partly because he may have legitimately thought they were going over the line and it was the right thing to bring them down.

The problem was: None of the undergraduates, including Ronnie Winston, would implicate them before the authorities at Harvard. The way Weil got the story for the Harvard Crimson was that he approached Ronnie Winston's parents. Ronnie Winston came from the Harry Winston diamond family. **Weil told his parents: "If Ronnie doesn't step forward and admit this, then we're going to put his name in the news story we're planning to publish about this."**

The parents thought they could keep Ronnie's name out of the story by making him come forward to the Harvard authorities—and that's what Ronnie did. Ronnie's admission is what gave Harvard "the goods" on Alpert and allowed them to fire him.

DAVID: I love the line this defiant kid, Ronnie Winston, delivers to the Harvard dean when he's forced to admit what happened.

DON: The dean asks, "Did you take drugs from Dr. Alpert?"

Ronnie says, "Yes sir, I did. And it was the most educational experience I've had at Harvard!"

Well, it all came out in a Page 1 news story in the Crimson with Weil's byline along with a vicious editorial attacking Leary and Alpert that called them things like "a virus" and "quacks." It was in the New York Times the next day.

Of course, now Andrew Weil is this Mr. Natural, this Oprah with a beard. In a way, he wound up replacing Leary and Alpert as a straight guy who knows how to get stoned naturally. He winds up becoming a leading light in the drug culture himself.

DAVID: We've just summarized some of the biggest news readers will discover in your book. And, there's a whole lot more! You actually invite readers into these dramatic scenes as the big story unfolds. So, finally, let's touch on Timothy Leary himself. He's also a major figure in this new book. So much has been published about him that I'm guessing there's not a lot of new insights into Leary himself in this book, right?

DON: I don't think I've revealed anything new on Leary. I definitely bring out a lot of new information on the other main characters, but a lot has been   published   on   Leary.
DAVID: After your own research on Leary, how do you feel about him, overall?

DON: A lot of people who write about Leary or knew Leary have a love-hate response to the guy. And I wound up with that same idea about him. He was one of the most revered and reviled people in the 1960s counterculture—including people **within** the counterculture.

Some people thought he was a prophet and a brilliant explorer of human consciousness. A lot of people thought he was a con artist.

Late in life, he was asked: "Well who are you?"

And he said: "You get the Timothy Leary you deserve."

That's why I call him "the Trickster" in this book, because people project their own ideas onto Leary. He's definitely the least sympathetic of the four main characters but Leary was kind of the mouth. He said things a lot of people were feeling who had taken psychedelic drugs—he articulated

259

things others couldn't or wouldn't say—and that's why he was considered so dangerous by the Nixon administration. Nixon called him "the most dangerous man in America," to which Leary replied: "Oh yeah? I have America surrounded!"

How can you not enjoy a guy who can come up with lines like that?

DAVID: You're reporting and writing a largely unknown history. You're telling us how some of our major spiritual figures came into such prominence today.

DON: The one who has the most obvious impact is Andrew Weil. He's done so much to bring together the best of Eastern and Western medicine. He's had a real impact on people's lives in the way we try to maintain our health and well-being. He's set up this center at the University of Arizona and now medical schools all across the country have programs based on ideas he pioneered in his work. He was way ahead of his time in getting mainstream medicine to rethink itself.

He's not proud of what he did back then at Harvard and he tried for years to apologize to Leary and Alpert for what happened to them. I think Leary did forgive him before he died.

ANDREW THOMAS WEIL

1963

Andrew Weil gave Harvard President Nathan Pusey the ammunition to get rid of Leary and Alpert. Weil, had wanted to volunteer as one of the psilocybin research subjects, but was rejected because Leary and Alpert had agreed to give the powerful mushroom pills only to graduate students, not undergraduates.

The following clip was found in the papers of Leary that tells of how two undergraduate (one of which was Weil) came to them and asked to be part of the psilocybin study.

> In the fall of 1961 members of our research group were approached by and met twice with several young men who have been informally experimenting with conscious-altering substances. All of these young men were or had been Harvard undergraduates. They wanted to talk with us about their experience, and particularly about their plans for a model free community in Mexico. Two of these young men did go to Mexico to look for a location, but they returned to Cambridge, To our knowledge no community has been established. In our discussions with these men we found them to be imaginative, decent, and full of youthful exuberance. We did nothing to encourage their use of conscious-altering substances. Rather, we expressed concern about the clandestine atmosphere in which they used these substances and talked very frankly with them about the frightening experiences that stem from secretiveness, suspicion, and fear.

But Weil became jealous when he learned that one of his undergraduate dorm mates, Ronnie Winston, had been let into the fold by Professor Alpert. At the time, Alpert was a gay man living in the closet. He would later admit that a romantic infatuation for the undergraduate clouded his judgment. Andy Weil went to Ronnie Winston's father, the celebrated jeweler Harry Winston, and threatened to publish his son's name in an expose he was writing for the Harvard Crimson—unless Ronnie would inform on Professor Alpert. So, under pressure from his father, Andy Weil and the Crimson, Ronnie was called into the dean's office and asked, "Did you take drugs from Professor Alpert." "Yes, sir, I did," Ronnie confessed, "and it was the most educational experience I'd had at Harvard." Alpert, a professor on tenure.

Timothy Leary's Legacy and the Rebirth of Psychedelic Research, *Don Lattin*

The firing of Timothy Leary and Richard Alpert from Harvard University is often inaccurately attributed to an article published in the *Harvard Crimson* by Andrew Weil, a Harvard student at the time, who would later become one of the university's leading researchers on psychedelics. This narrative has been perpetuated in various accounts, including early 2010 articles in *The New York Times* discussing Don Lattin's book *The Harvard Psychedelic Club*. These articles suggest that Weil's piece was the catalyst for the dismissal of the two prominent psychologists. However, the facts tell a different story.

In reality, Andrew Weil's article, published on May 28, 1963, had no bearing on the firings of Leary and Alpert. By the time the article appeared, Leary had already left the university, and Alpert was in the process of clearing out his office. The true reasons for their dismissal were rooted in a growing backlash that had been building since at least May 1961, with various influential Harvard professors voicing concerns over the pair's controversial experiments with psychedelic substances.

The portrayal of Weil's article as the turning point oversimplifies a complex situation. Leary and Alpert's work had long drawn criticism and suspicion from the academic community, especially due to their involvement in administering psilocybin to students. Their unconventional research methods and increasing notoriety within and outside the university had made their positions untenable long before Weil's article was published.

This timeline reveals that the firings were the culmination of years of mounting tension rather than a direct result of a single student's article.

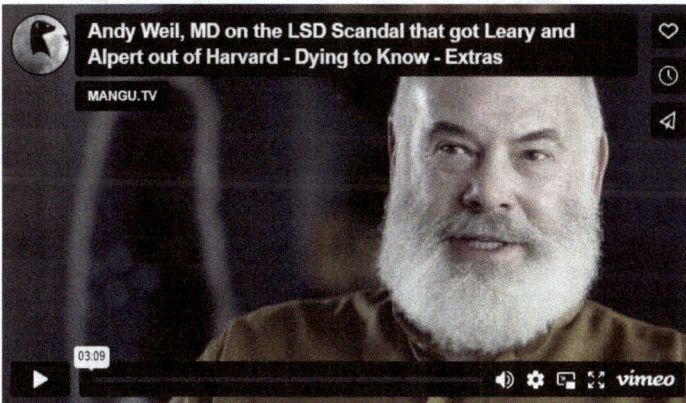

https://www.youtube.com/watch?v=BZyjIpQWJzo

At a meeting of the
President and Fellows of Harvard College
in Cambridge, May 6, 1963

Voted, because Timothy F. Leary, Lecturer on
Clinical Psychology, has failed to keep his classroom
appointments and has absented himself from Cambridge
during term time without permission, to relieve him
from further teaching duty and to terminate his salary
as of April 30, 1963.

A true copy of record,

Attest:

Secretary

Dr. Timothy F. Leary

264

The Reunion, 20 Years Later

The Harvard Crimson

The University Daily Est. 1873

NO WRITER ATTRIBUTED

April 23, 1983

In 1962. Harvard fired two controversial young psychologists from their Faculty posts following a year of tumult about the pair's research on LSD and other hallucinogenic drugs. Tomorrow both men will return to Harvard Timothy Leary whose "turn on tune in and drop out" became the rallying cry for a generation of drugs-users, and Richard Alpert who now goes by the name Ram Dass.

The two will speak at Sanders Theater at 10:30 a.m. in an event being billed as a "psychedelic reunion".

The forum will be moderated by Professor of Psychology David C. McCelland, who chaired the now-defunct Social Relations Department at the time of the controversy.

The New York Times

PUBLISH DATE - April 25, 1983

Leary Lectures at Harvard For First Time in 20 Years

CAMBRIDGE, Mass., April 24 (AP) — For the first time since his dismissal from Harvard 20 years ago for experimenting with mind-altering drugs, Timothy Leary returned today to praise the university as the "big league of chemical psychedelic experimentation."

"Since the day we were canned, I never have felt any rancor against Harvard," Mr. Leary told a full house at Memorial Hall. "Harvard is the main line of American transcendental thinking."

Mr. Leary, a former lecturer, appeared with Richard Alpert, 49 years old, an assistant clinical psychology professor who was dismissed with him in May 1963. The university contended that they broke an agreement against using undergraduates in drug experiments.

"The problem, was, of course, the world wasn't ready for us," Mr. Leary said.

No Regrets for One

"I think they were," Mr. Alpert interjected. "Not for one moment

do I wish I was not thrown out of Harvard."

Both men were introduced by Dr. David Clarence McClelland, a psychology professor who headed the Center for Research in Personality where they did research. He said in 1962 that he feared the permanent effects of their experiments.

Mr. Leary, 62, contended that Harvard had always attracted scholars interested in drugs and the mind, and had always been in the "mainstream tradition of far-out, Sufi, gnostic, Harvard experimentation."

He also asserted that in the 1950's the Central Intelligence Agency placed ads in the campus newspaper to recruit Harvard students to participate in experiments with mind-altering drugs.

Student Promoted Lecture

Joseph A. Kasof, a Harvard graduate student in sociology, said he promoted the lecture because of his interest in psychedelic drugs. He hired the hall and security force and paid for advertising at a total

cost of about $2,300, he said.

Tickets were $3, and crowds of students stood outside in the rain asking for extras.

Mr. Kasof said that the speakers agreed to appear for no fee but that he planned to split any profits with them.

Richard Alpert, left, and Timothy Leary at Harvard University.

United Press International

Timothy Leary, David McClelland, and Ram Dass (Richard Alpert), 1983

266

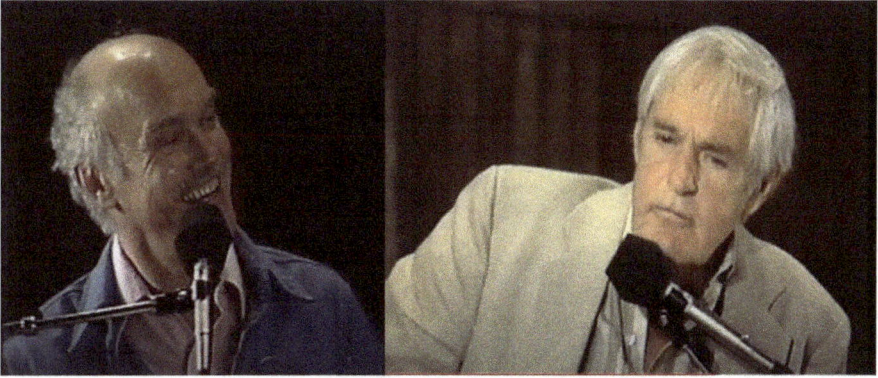

Richard Alpert (Ram Dass) and Timothy Leary

PSYCHEDELIC REUNION!

DR. TIMOTHY
LEARY & DR. RICHARD
("Ram Dass")
ALPERT
RETURN TO HARVARD!

SUNDAY, APRIL 24 - 10:30 A.M.
Sanders Theatre, Harvard University

Listen to the evening talk

https://soundcloud.com/thebeezone/timothy-leary-and-ram-das-harvard-reunion-1983?si=35361e1d6d0a4737b419ebe7ee7879f3&utm_source=clipboard&utm_medium=text&utm_campaign=social_sharing

Richard Alpert and Timothy Leary 'After Thoughts'

Agree to Disagree

After Reunion Event

Ram Dass and Timothy Leary 'After Show'

https://youtu.be/eYs-qohH6O8?si=qHPCn6wxucxaqSPL

The Crazy Aftermath

War on Drugs

"The Most Dangerous Man in America"

June 17, 1971: In a press conference, President Nixon declares drug abuse "public enemy number one."

June 17, 1971: In a press conference, President Nixon declares drug abuse "public enemy number one." He announces the creation of a special action office for drug abuse prevention and requests $155 million to underwrite the effort, $105 million of which would be dedicated to treatment and rehabilitation.

269

AUTHOR INTERVIEWS

Nixon's Manhunt For The High Priest Of LSD In 'The Most Dangerous Man In America'

January 5, 2018 · 4:17 PM ET
Heard on All Things Considered

👤 Ari Shapiro

▶ **8-Minute Listen**   + PLAYLIST ⬇ ⟨⟩ ☰

Dr. Timothy Leary, an advocate for LSD, working at his desk.
Hulton Archive/Getty Images

Prohibition to Revival

1970 - 1995

"I realized people were not having (psychedelic) experiences; they were having experiences of themselves.

But they were coming from depths that psychoanalysis didn't know anything about." — Stanislav Grof

Stanislav Grof, M.D., (stanislavgrof.com) Psychiatrist

***

"There was no legal LSD in this country after 1966. So there are about 7 or 8 million people who took bathtub LSD or garage LSD or bootleg LSD. And if they were lucky, they got something that was reasonably good, but most of it was laced with speed or God knows what. This was a cause of tremendous concern to us. "

'Fresh Air' Reflects On The Psychedelic Movement, October 23, 2020, A 1983 interview with psychologist Timothy Leary

In 1986, a seminal year in the annals of psychedelic research, the Multidisciplinary Association for Psychedelic Studies (MAPS) came into existence. MAPS - The establishment of MAPS marked a turning point, as it was instrumental in compelling government agencies to shift their stance, albeit slowly. This transformation unfolded in stages, with initial research focusing on animal studies with psychedelic chemicals.

It wasn't until the mid to late 1990s that the research landscape began to see glimmers of a revival of psychedelic exploration. Human studies were cautiously initiated during this period, signifying a critical milestone in understanding these substances' medical and scientific benefits. However,

271

it's essential to acknowledge that this resurgence was far from a universal and legally uncomplicated affair.

The research, now allowed within the narrow confines of the law, was fraught with limitations. Time-consuming bureaucratic procedures and significant costs often characterize it. Nevertheless, this marked the embryonic stage of the resurgence of psychedelic research, offering hope for a more comprehensive understanding of these substances and their potential contributions to human well-being.

Search

Psychedelic and Dissociative Drugs

En español

Highlights

- Psychedelic and dissociative drugs can temporarily alter a person's mood, thoughts, and perceptions. Among other health effects and safety concerns, people who use these substances report feeling strong emotions ranging from bliss to fear and experiencing vast changes in how they perceive reality.

- In recent years, there has been growing research interest in the potential of psychedelic and dissociative drugs to treat medical conditions, including mental health disorders. An increasing number of people also report taking these drugs outside of medical settings for recreation, to improve well-being, or for spiritual or self-exploration.

- NIDA supports and conducts research to better understand the health effects of psychedelic and dissociative drugs and to learn whether some of these drugs may help treat substance use disorders in medical settings.

273

Jordan Peterson with Roland Griffiths

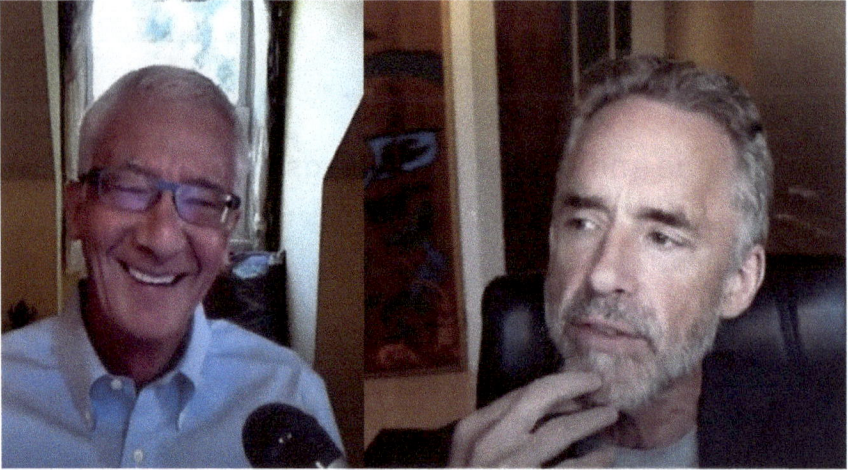

https://www.youtube.com/watch?v=zlNti4uDMr0

May 10, 2021

Roland Griffiths ventured out from traditional clinical research into the mysterious world of Psychedelic Sciences; a study that has continued to excite him decades later. A scientist by training, he approached the psychedelics with what he calls extreme skepticism, but the transformative effects of Psilocybin in his first research participants sent him on a career trajectory that has changed the entire field.

AUTHOR INTERVIEWS

'Fresh Air' Reflects On The Psychedelic Movement

October 23, 2020 · 1:35 PM ET
Heard on Fresh Air

Terry Gross

FRESH AIR

▶ **39-Minute Listen**   + PLAYLIST ⬇ <> ☰

We listen to a 1983 interview with psychologist Timothy Leary, a 1990 interview with spiritual leader Ram Dass and a 2018 interview with *How to Change Your Mind* author Michael Pollan.

· · ·

Following the enactment of the Drug Abuse Control Amendment (1965) and the Controlled Substances Act (1970), psychedelic drugs were effectively criminalized, driving their production, distribution, and use underground. This sweeping legislative move had unintended consequences, giving rise to a clandestine subculture of otherwise upstanding and law-abiding citizens who viewed these substances as beneficial, often transformative, and even life-changing.

In essence, the government's actions inadvertently thrust into existence an underground and outlawed community comprised of individuals who, by and large, were respected members of society. These individuals, driven by

275

a sincere belief in the therapeutic potential of psychedelics, chose to defy the law to access what they considered vital tools for personal growth and mental well-being.

Notably, the historical context of psychedelic substances provides a fascinating lens through which to understand this phenomenon. In ancient times, these same substances, now labeled as "drugs," were recognized for their profound psychological effects and spiritual significance. In those eras, they were often referred to as mystical or sacred medicines, illustrating their role in enhancing well-being at an individual level and within the broader societal context.

Intriguingly, these substances were embraced for their potential to facilitate transformative experiences, introspection, and connections to the spiritual realm. Communities often incorporated them into rituals and ceremonies, acknowledging their profound impact on the human psyche and overall spiritual growth.

As these ancient practices have been labeled "drug use" in contemporary times, the stigma associated with them has grown, inadvertently criminalizing the substances themselves and the individuals who continue to seek their potential benefits.

It is clear that medical and psychological research into these strange agents, at a painfully embryonic state at the present time, promises more than we are able fully to comprehend. *Powerful new tools for psychiatry may be only one of the results of such investigations. But research into the effects of these substances on the human mind must be carried out carefully, without haste or superficiality and, above all, by the most qualified personnel, for what may be one of the most promising fields for progress ever within man's grasp can easily be jeopardized or utterly destroyed by irresponsible and inadequately planned research or by the manipulations of dilettantes.*

276

The Harvard Project Today

Prescription, medicine, and Drugs

A Game of Words

The NEW ENGLAND JOURNAL of MEDICINE

Perspective
NOVEMBER 9, 2023

How Should the FDA Evaluate Psychedelic Medicine?

Mason Marks, M.D., J.D., and I. Glenn Cohen, J.D.

Drug companies are spending millions of dollars to incorporate psychedelic agents into health care.[1] Working with research institutions, patient organizations, and veterans groups, they have gained bipartisan support in Congress. Meanwhile, mounting clinical evidence is paving the way for the likely approval of new psychedelic medicines by the Food and Drug Administration (FDA).

FDA review is important because psychedelics are Schedule I controlled substances, which means the Drug Enforcement Ad-

preparing to prescribe psychedelics. But several of its recommendations may be contentious.

Psychedelics produce changes in cognition, perception, and affect. The guidance recognizes that some psychedelics, such as lysergic acid diethylamide (LSD), will be synthesized, and others may be botanical drugs consisting of plant or fungal material, such as

stress disorder (PTSD), it might accelerate research on new indications.

The guidance discusses limitations associated with blinding in placebo-controlled psychedelics trials. Because psychedelics produce perceptual changes, participants and researchers can often identify the groups to which participants are assigned, which could potentially bias study results. The FDA proposes minimizing "functional unblinding" by administering subperceptual doses of psychedelics or other substances whose effects mimic

What is a Cure?

Middle English (as a noun): from Old French curer (verb), cure (noun), both from Latin curare 'take care of', from cura 'care'. The original noun senses were 'care, concern, responsibility', in particular, spiritual care (hence cure (sense 3 of the noun)). In late Middle English the senses 'medical care' and 'successful medical treatment' arose, and hence 'remedy'.

Google image search for the term "medicine"

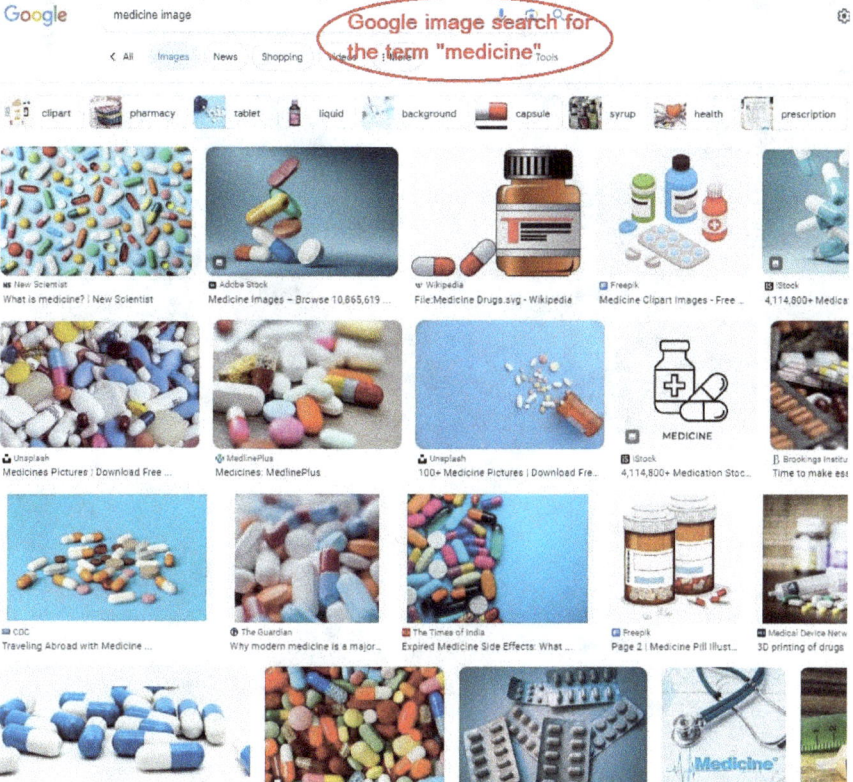

PSYCHEDELICS AND HARVARD TODAY

Harvard Law

Harvard Medical School

HARVARD DIVINITY SCHOOL

February 19, 2022

The Harvard Crimson

The University Daily Est. 1873

At Harvard, Psychedelic Drugs' Tentative Renaissance

"The Center for the Neuroscience of Psychedelics aims to understand the mechanisms underlying psychedelics' effects on the brain with a variety of methods; one lab in the group studies the neurochemistry underlying their function, and another branch focuses on functional MRI studies."

In the early 1960s, the Harvard Psilocybin Project made national headlines for its unethical research methods and controversial leader, psychologist Timothy F. Leary. Now, sixty years after Leary's departure, Harvard is again part of the conversation around the future of psychedelics. From research in the lab to conversations among the student body, psychedelics are making a tentative yet undeniable renaissance on campus — a renaissance conscious of Harvard's checkered history with the substances, yet working to move beyond it.

Now, after a decades-long pause, psychedelics research is reemerging at some of the country's most well-respected academic institutions — including at Harvard.

Jerry F. Rosenbaum, a professor of Psychiatry at Harvard Medical School who has served as chair of the MGH Psychiatry department for 20 years, leads the new Center for the Neuroscience of Psychedelics at MGH, founded in April 2021. The center is one of several psychedelic research centers — including at Johns Hopkins, UC Berkeley, and NYU — that have opened in recent years.

Rosenbaum became interested in the subject after attending a conference on psychedelics at the Broad Institute, where he heard a talk on how psychedelics affect the same pathway of the brain implicated in rumination, a phenomenon associated with depression and anxiety. Hoping that psychedelics could be the key to helping his depressed and anxious patients, Rosenbaum decided to launch the center to conduct further research.

"I don't remember that it occurred to me that anybody would object to it," Rosenbaum says about the Center's founding. "So I didn't really ask for permission. We just did it."

Promising early evidence about the drugs' efficacy has largely eroded lingering fears from the '60s about addiction and overdose potential. In addition to treating PTSD, psychedelics have been shown to aid treatment of other disorders, including depression, where they reduced symptoms in 71 percent of patients. Similarly, psychedelics have also been shown to help with anxiety, opioid and nicotine addiction, alcohol abuse, and OCD.

"Given what seemed the inevitability of psychedelics, it was clearly our responsibility and mission to get involved and understand them better," Rosenbaum says.

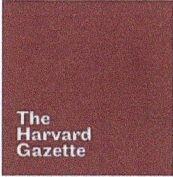

DATE: October 16, 2023

NEWS +

News from Harvard schools, offices, and affiliates

Harvard launches new Study of Psychedelics in Society and Culture

John Harvard Statue in Harvard Yard.
Stephanie Mitchell/Harvard Staff
Photographer

Harvard Medical School

All Articles > Altering Perceptions on Psychedelics

Spring 2022

Altering Perceptions on Psychedelics

Growing evidence for the safety and efficacy of psychedelics could lead to better treatments for anxiety, depression, pain, and other often intractable conditions

Viral World Issue

by Allison Eck —— ⏱ 15 minute read

A lithograph of *Champignons Suspects* drawn by A. Cornillon for Michel Etienne Descourtilz's 1827 taxonomic text on mushroom species found in Haiti. *Atlas des champignons: comestibles, suspects et veneneux.*

New center seeks to understand any 'magic' in mushrooms

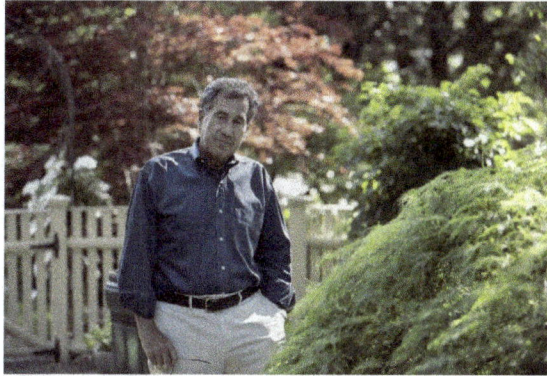

Research may help clear path for use of psychedelics in treating psychiatric patients

Media Mentions - Research News

Altering Our Perceptions of the Psychedelics (Harvard Medicine)

July 7, 2022

By Ruta Nonacs, MD PhD

Moving beyond the 1960s counterculture, psychedelics, including psilocybin and MDMA, have emerged as promising novel treatments for depression and other psychiatric disorders. Research indicates that these psychedelic compounds may promote neuroplasticity, creating a unique opportunity to change patterns in brain activity, and in turn, improve symptoms, behavior and functioning.

Last year the Mass General launched a new program, the Center for the Neuroscience of Psychedelics. This is a collaborative endeavor including researchers from the Department of Psychiatry, the Chemical Neurobiology Laboratory, and the Athinoula A. Martinos Center for Biomedical Imaging. The Center seeks to understand how

> *We really want to understand what is happening in the brain, from molecular to cellular to network and beyond. What happens that allows people to improve and recover?*

Legalizing MDMA for PTSD Treatment: Phase 3 Clinical Trial Results

by **KATIE BROWN**   *MAY 23, 2023 AT 11:05 AM UTC*

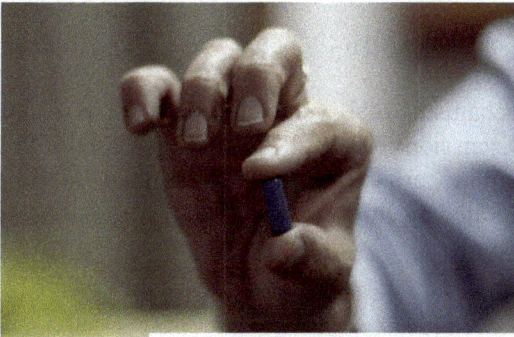

MOST POPULAR

SYSTEMATIC REVIEW

Systematic Review of Psychiatric Observation Units and Their Impact on Emergency Department Boarding

Psychiatric observation units are mainly described within large urban general or academic hospital centers. Patients present predominantly with acute mental health crises or suicidality and are typically treated < 72 hours.

Prim Care Companion CNS Disord 2023;25(6):22r03468

Alastair W. Magarey and others

289

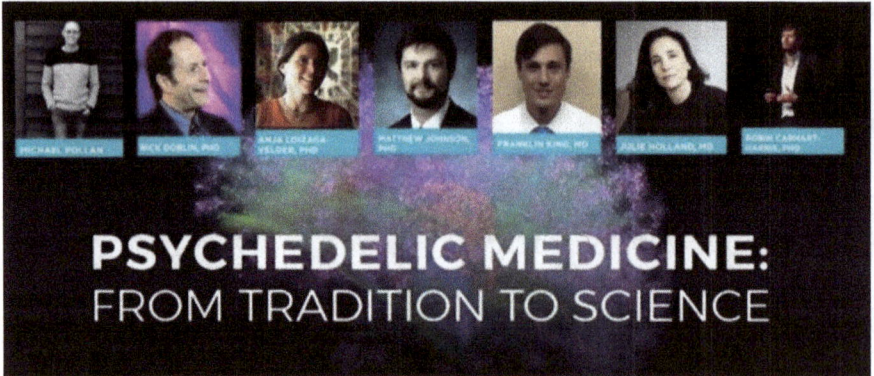

PSYCHEDELIC MEDICINE:
FROM TRADITION TO SCIENCE

https://www.youtube.com/watch?v=SwMHr43fTqE

Lecture: The Therapeutic Mechanisms of Psychedelic Medicine by Robin Carhart-Harris, PhD Panel Discussion: Michael Pollan Rick Doblin, PhD Anja Loizaga-Velder, PhD Robin Carhart-Harris, PhD Matthew Johnson, PhD Franklin King, MD Moderated by Julie Holland, MD

Harvard Law School

Harvard Law School Launches First-Ever Research Initiative on Psychedelics and the Law

The Petrie-Flom Center for Health Law Policy, Biotechnology, and Bioethics at Harvard Law School studies the law and policy around health care. By Truong L. Nguyen

By Emmy M. Cho, Crimson Staff Writer

July 2, 2021

Harvard Law School's Petrie-Flom Center for Health Law Policy, Biotechnology, and Bioethics is launching a first-of-its-kind research initiative focused on psychedelics and the law, the center announced Wednesday.

Titled the Project on Psychedelics Law and Regulation, the three-year project will "promote safety, innovation, equity, and access" in both psychedelic research and treatment, according to a press release.

"POPLAR is the first academic initiative focused on psychedelics law and policy, positioned to be the global leader for research and education in this space," the release reads.

The Project on Psychedelics Law and Regulation (POPLAR)

The Petrie-Flom Center for Health Law Policy, Biotechnology, and Bioethics at Harvard Law School is engaged in a three-year initiative to examine the ethical, legal, and social implications of psychedelics research, commerce, and therapeutics. Launched in summer 2021 with a generous grant from the Saisei Foundation, *the Project on Psychedelics Law and Regulation (POPLAR) at the Petrie-Flom Center for Health Law Policy, Biotechnology, and Bioethics at Harvard Law School* will advance evidence-based psychedelics law and policy.

Background

Despite a longstanding prohibition on psychedelics dating back to the 1970s, scientific and public interest in these substances is growing. Clinical trials repeatedly demonstrate their promise for treating mood, anxiety, and substance use disorders.

In 2017, the FDA designated MDMA a breakthrough therapy for post-traumatic stress disorder, and in 2018 the agency identified psilocybin as a breakthrough for treatment-resistant depression. These developments indicate that psychedelics may represent substantial improvements over existing treatments for mental illness.

While psychedelic therapies make their way through the drug development pipeline, seven U.S. cities and the State of Oregon have decriminalized them, and last November, Oregon voters legalized the supervised administration of psilocybin. At least eight other states are considering similar legislation to legalize or decriminalize psychedelics.

Due to their therapeutic and commercial potential, the U.S. market for psychedelics is projected to reach $6.85 billion by 2027, attracting a significant number of for-profit companies and investors. However, despite the proliferation of clinical research centers, increasing private investment in psychedelic drug development, and widespread state and local decriminalization, there is a relative lack of research on the ethical, legal, and social implications of psychedelics research, commerce, and therapeutics.

POPLAR will focus on promoting safety, innovation, and equity in psychedelics research, commerce, and therapeutics.

Project research will focus on the following key areas:

- Ethics in Psychedelics Research and Therapeutics
- Challenges at the Intersection of Psychedelics and Intellectual Property Law
- Opportunities for Federal Support of Psychedelics Research
- Access to Psychedelic Therapies and Equity in Emerging Psychedelics Industries
- The Role of Psychedelics in Healing Trauma

I. Glenn Cohen

Faculty Director, James A. Attwood and Leslie Williams Professor of Law, and Deputy Dean

✉ email
👤 Profile Page

⊙ Curriculum Vitae
↗ Follow Glenn on Twitter.
↗ Follow Glenn on SSRN.

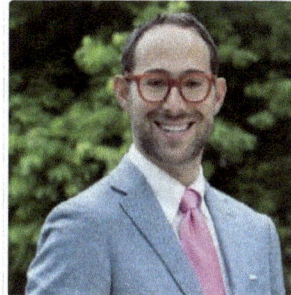

I. Glenn Cohen

Prof. Cohen is one of the world's leading experts on the intersection of bioethics (sometimes also called "medical ethics") and the law, as well as health law. He also teaches civil procedure. From Seoul to Krakow to Vancouver, Professor Cohen has spoken at legal, medical, and industry conferences around the world and his work has appeared in or been covered on PBS, NPR, ABC, CNN, MSNBC, Mother Jones, the New York Times, the New Republic, the Boston Globe, and several other media venues.

He was the youngest professor on the faculty at Harvard Law School (tenured or untenured) both when he joined the faculty in 2008 (at age 29) and when he was tenured as a full professor in 2013 (at age 34), though not the youngest in history.

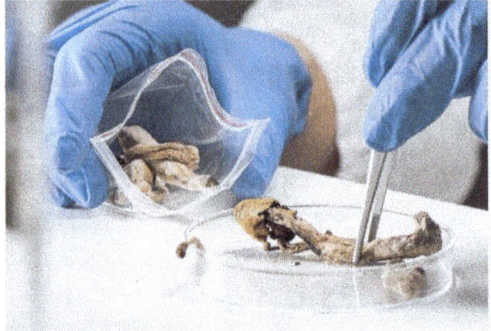

A Q&A with Mason Marks on new psychedelics law and regulation initiative

By Chloe Reichel

Credit: Getty Images/iStockphoto

On June 30, the Petrie-Flom Center announced the launch of a three-year research initiative, the Project on Psychedelics Law and Regulation (POPLAR), which is supported by a generous grant from the Saisei Foundation.

The Project on Psychedelics Law and Regulation at the Petrie-Flom Center for Health Law Policy, Biotechnology, and Bioethics at Harvard Law School will advance evidence-based psychedelics law and policy.

Mason Marks is an assistant professor of law at the University of New Hampshire Franklin Pierce School of Law. He is a senior fellow and project lead of the Project on Psychedelics Law and Regulation (POPLAR) at the Petrie-Flom Center for Health Law Policy, Biotechnology, and Bioethics at Harvard Law School.

THE PETRIE-FLOM CENTER
FOR HEALTH LAW POLICY, BIOTECHNOLOGY,
AND BIOETHICS AT HARVARD LAW SCHOOL

| Events | Research | Fellows | Blog | JLB | Resources | For Students | About |

Fellows — Postdoctoral Fellows

Mason Marks

Senior Fellow and Project Lead on the Project on Psychedelics Law and Regulation at the Petrie-Flom Center for Health Law Policy, Biotechnology, and Bioethics at Harvard Law School

✉ email
👤 Profile Page
Mason Marks' SSRN Page.

Dr. Mason Marks is the Florida Bar Health Law Section Professor at the Florida State University College of Law. At Harvard Law School, he is the senior fellow and project lead of the Project on Psychedelics Law and Regulation (POPLAR) at the Petrie-Flom Center for Health Law Policy, Biotechnology, and Bioethics. He is also an affiliated fellow at the Information Society Project (ISP) at Yale Law School. Marks was previously a fellow-in-residence at the Edmond J. Safra Center for Ethics at Harvard University, a research scholar at the Information Law Institute at NYU Law School, and a visiting fellow at Yale Law School's ISP.

Mason Marks

A Q&A with Mason Marks on new psychedelics law and regulation initiative

By Chloe Reichel

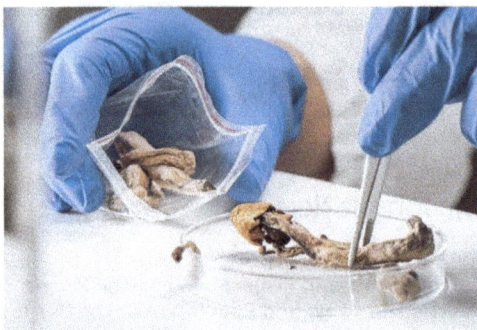
Credit: Getty Images/iStockphoto

On June 30, the Petrie-Flom Center announced the launch of a three-year research initiative, the Project on Psychedelics Law and Regulation (POPLAR), which is supported by a generous grant from the Saisei Foundation.

The Project on Psychedelics Law and Regulation at the Petrie-Flom Center for Health Law Policy, Biotechnology, and Bioethics at Harvard Law School will advance evidence-based psychedelics law and policy.

HARVARD DIVINITY SCHOOL

CENTER FOR THE STUDY
OF WORLD RELIGIONS

About   News and Events   **Research and Programming**   Openings, Appointments, and Grants   Residence

**RESEARCH AND
PROGRAMMING**

HOME / RESEARCH AND PROGRAMMING / TRANSCENDENCE AND TRANSFORMATION /

**˅ Transcendence
and
Transformation**

Research

Gnoseologies

**PSYCHEDELICS
AND THE FUTURE
OF RELIGION**

Reading Groups &
Workshops

Database

Pop Apocalypse
Podcast

Annual Lectures

Psychedelics and the Future of Religion

"What do psychedelics, entheogens, and plant medicines have to do with religion and spirituality, in the past, present, and future? This series, now in its third year, aims to pursue this question rigorously and responsibly, balancing curiosity with critique, exploration with evidence. Topics have included: psychedelic science's investment in quantifying "mystical" experience; psychedelic chaplaincy; the question of psychedelics in the ancient Mediterranean and Near East; indigenous plant medicine traditions, ancient and modern; peyote conservation efforts among the Native American Church and their legal challenges; and more besides (see the videos below). Many more topics remain to be explored, including the racial dynamics of the psychedelic underground, psychedelic exceptionalism, psychedelics and metaphysics, and the role of spirituality in psychedelic psychiatry. In the 2023-24 year, this series will coordinate with the student-led working group, "Psychedelics, Sacred and Subversive."

And many more topics remain to be explored. In the 2023-24 year, this series will coordinate with the student-led reading group, Psychedelics: Sacred and Subversive: A reading and learning group exploring the altering of religion.

CENTER FOR THE STUDY OF WORLD RELIGIONS

About   News and Events   Research and Programming   Openings, Appointments, and Grants   Residence

Charles M. Stang

Director of the Center for the Study of World Religions
Professor of Early Christian Thought

Charles Stang joined the Faculty of Divinity in 2008. His research and teaching focus on the history and theology of Christianity in late antiquity, especially Eastern varieties of Christianity. More specifically, he is interested in the development of asceticism, monasticism, and mysticism in Eastern Christianity.

His most recent book, *Our Divine Double*, was published in 2016 by Harvard University Press. His earlier book, *Apophasis and Pseudonymity in Dionysius the Areopagite: "No Longer I"* (Oxford University Press, 2012), won the Manfred Lautenschläger Award for Theological Promise in 2013. Stang is also editor of *The Waking Dream of T.E. Lawrence: Essays on His Life, Literature, and Legacy* (Palgrave, 2002); with Sarah Coakley, *Rethinking Dionysius the Areopagite* (Wiley-Blackwell, 2009); and with Zachary Guiliano, *The Open Body: Essays in Anglican Ecclesiology* (Peter Lang, 2012).

Archives of the Impossible conference | Plenary Lecture: Charles M. Stang

https://www.youtube.com/watch?v=dzaSlubrVxY&t=2s

301

Charles M. Stang, professor of Early Christian Thought and the director of the Center for the Study of World Religions (CSWR) at Harvard Divinity School, lectured on "The Call of the Ancient: Psychedelic Pasts and Futures" during the international conference at Rice University titled "Archives of the Impossible: Transnationalism, Transdisciplinarity, Transcendence." The May 11-13, 2023 conference featured speakers and panelists who set out to demystify the paranormal through their research and experiences regarding metaphysics, UFOs and much more.

CENTER FOR THE STUDY OF WORLD RELIGIONS

About   News and Events   Research and Programming   Openings, Appointments, and Grants   Residence

News

Calendar

Past Events

Video: Psychedelics and the Future of Religion: Race and Exoticism in Global Psychedelic Spirituality

November 7, 2023

As part of the Psychedelics and the Future of Religion series, the Center for the Study of World Religions hosted scholars Dr. Amanda Lucia, Professor of Religious Studies at the University of California-Riverside and Dr. Arun Saldanha, Professor in the Department of Geography, Environment, and Society at the University of Minnesota for a discussion on "**Race and Exoticism in Global Psychedelic Spirituality**".

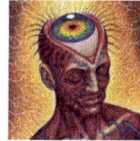

Drawing from their respective perspectives and scholarship, Professors Lucia and Saldanha discussed the racialized politics/ethics of the hallucinogenic experience (or discourses thereof) within the context of modern spiritualities.

303

Psychedelics, Spirituality, and a Culture of Seekership

May 12, 2022

In 2022, conversations about the connections between psychedelics, science and medicine, and spirituality are again top of mind, from Harvard and the academy to research hospitals and beyond. / Art design by Kristie Welsh

You're listening to the Harvard Religion Beat, and my name is Paul Gillis-Smith, a correspondent for the Divinity School....read more >>>

S

CENTER FOR THE STUDY OF WORLD RELIGIONS

Video: Psychedelics and the Future of Religion: Race and Exoticism in Global Psychedelic Spirituality

November 7, 2023

As part of the Psychedelics and the Future of Religion series, the Center for the Study of World Religions hosted scholars Dr. Amanda Lucia, Professor of Religious Studies at the University of California-Riverside and Dr. Arun Saldanha, Professor in the Department of Geography, Environment, and Society at the University of Minnesota for a discussion on **"Race and Exoticism in Global Psychedelic Spirituality"**.

Drawing from their respective perspectives and scholarship, Professors Lucia and Saldanha discussed the racialized politics/ethics of the hallucinogenic experience (or discourses thereof) within the context of modern spiritualities.

305

Event Detail

Plant (and Fungi!) Consciousness Reading Group

When	Thursday, November 16, 2023, 12 – 2pm
Where	CSWR Conference Room, 42 Francis Ave, Cambridge, MA 02138
Programming Series	Transcendence and Transformation
Sponsor	Center for the Study of World Religions at Harvard Divinity School
Contact	Natalia Schwien, nataliaschwien@fas.harvard.edu & Rachael Petersen, rpetersen@hds.harvard.edu
Details	Do plants think? Do fungi dream? What can the more-than-human world teach us about the nature of mind?
	Recent scientific research has shed light on the sophisticated ways in which plants and fungi sense, make sense of, and interact with the world. Alongside these discoveries is a wave of interest in the "more-than-human" humanities. This scholarship raises fundamental questions about the nature of the human and the non-human: what is mind, where does it extend, and how? What is matter, and what does it mean to label it "animate" or

Panel Discussion:

Michael Pollan, Rick Doblin, PhD Anja Loizaga-Velder,

PhD Robin Carhart-Harris, PhD Matthew Johnson, PhD Franklin King, MD

306

Bibliography

Books and Collections

- Das, Rameshwar. Being Ram Dass. Sounds True, 2021.

- Giffort, Danielle. Acid Revival. University of Minnesota Press, 2020.

- Hagenbach, Dieter, and Luius Werthmuller. Mystic Chemist. Synergetic Press, 2011.

- Hatsis, Thomas. LSD - The Wonder Child. Park Street Press, 2021.

- Lattin, Don. The Harvard Psychedelic Club. Harper One, 2011.

- Lee, Martin A., and Bruce Shlain. Acid Dreams. Grove Press, 1985.

- Leary, Timothy. Flashbacks. Putnam Press, 1983.

- Leary, Timothy. High Priest. Ronin Publishing, 1968.

- Muraresku, Brian C. The Immortality Key. St. Martin's Press, 2020.

- Pennen, James. Timothy Leary: The Harvard Years. Park Street Press, 2014.

- Smith, Huston. Cleansing the Doors of Perception: The Religious Significance of Entheogenic Plants and Chemicals. Tharcher, 2000.

- Soloman, David. LSD: The Consciousness-Expanding Drug. G.P. Putnam's Sons, 1966.

- Stevens, Jay. Storming Heaven. Grove Press, 1998.

307

Articles

- "A Social and Cultural History of the Federal Prohibition of Psilocybin." Dissertation for Doctor of Philosophy, Colin Wark, University of Missouri-Columbia, August 2007.

- "A Trip Down Memory Lane: LSD at Harvard." Harvard Crimson, Nathaniel J. Hiatt, May 23, 2016.

- "Acid Brothers - Henry Beecher, Timothy Leary and the Psychedelic of the Century." Jonathan Moreno, University of Pennsylvania.

- "Altered States: LSD and the Anesthesia Laboratory of Henry Knowles Beecher." George A. Mashour, University of Michigan Medical School.

- "Beecher Study - The Response of Normal Men to Lysergic Acid Derivatives Di and Mono Ethlamides - Correlation of Personality and Drug Reactions."

- "Botanical Sources of the New World Narcotics." Psychedelic Review, Richard Evans Schultes, vol. 1, no. 2, Fall 1963.

- "Brief Life of Henry Knowles Beecher." Harvard Magazine, 2017.

- "Dr. Leary's Concord Prison Experiment: A 34-Year Follow-Up Study." Rick Doblins, M.P.P.

- "Drugs Which Antagonize 5-Hydroxytryptamine." J. H. Gaddum and Khan A. Hameed, British Journal of Pharmacology and Chemotherapy, Department of Pharmacology, University of Edinburgh, March 29, 1954.

- "Enduring Contributions of Henry Beecher, MD to Medicine, Science and Society." Edited by Edward Lowenstein, W. Andrew Kofke, MD, and Buckman McPeek, University of Pennsylvania.

- "From LSD to IRB, Henry Beecher's Psychedelic Research and the Foundations of Clinical Ethics." George A. Mashour, University of Michigan Medical School.

- "Glossy Visions: Coverage of LSD in Popular Magazines, 1954-1968." Dissertation for Doctor of Philosophy, Stephen I. Siff, Scripps College of Communication, Ohio University, November 2008.

- "Hallucination Drug Fought at Harvard." Boston Globe, Noah Gordon, March 1962.

- "Harvard and the Making of the Unabomber." Alston Chase, The Atlantic, June 2000.

- "Harvard Explains Psychology Aims, Dr. Morton Prince." NY Times, May 2, 1926.

- "Harvard LSD Research Draws National Attention." Harvard Crimson, Nikita Kansra and Cynthia W. Shih, May 21, 2012.

- "I.F.I.F. Group Plans Center for Research, Drug Experimenters to Work in Mexico." Harvard Crimson, Joel E. Cohen, January 16, 1963.

- "Leary and Alpert Attach Monro Stand on Drugs." Harvard Crimson, December 11, 1962.

- "Leary Lectures at Harvard for First Time in 20 Years." NY Times, April 25, 1983.

- "Letter from Alpert, Leary." Harvard Crimson, December 13, 1962.

- "Observations from Richard Alpert - Early Interview."

- "Psychedelics and Entheogens: Implications of Administration in Medical and Non-Medical Contexts." Hannah Rae Kirk, Thesis, Oregon State University, Honors College, May 23, 2018.

- "Psychotomimetric Drugs." Henry K. Beecher, M.D., The Anesthesia Laboratory of the Harvard Medical School at the Massachusetts General Hospital, Boston, Mass., 1958.

- "Psilocybin Expert Raps Leary, Alpert on Drugs." Harvard Crimson, Efrem Sigel, December 12, 1962.

- "Psychic Research LSD." Time Magazine, Medicine, March 29, 1963.

- "Recollections of the Good Friday Experiment: An Interview with Huston Smith." Interviewed by Thomas B. Roberts and Robert N. Jesse, 1966.

- "Reflections on the Concord Prison Project and the Follow-Up Study." Ralph Metzner, Ph.D.

- "State Will Investigate Research on Psilocybin." Harvard Crimson, March 21, 1962.

- "Statement of the Purpose of the International Federation for Internal Freedom."

- "The Effects of Psychedelic Experience on Language Functioning." Stanley Drippner, Ph.D., Psychedelics.

- "The Harvard Review, vol. 1, no. 4, Summer 1963." Josiah Lee Auspitz, Harvard Review, May 27, 1963.

- "The Hallucinogenic Mushrooms of Mexico and Psilocybin: A Bibliography." R. Gordon Wasson, Botanical Museum Leaflets, Harvard University, March 10, 1963.

- "The Strange Case of the Harvard Drug Scandal." Andrew T. Weil, Look Magazine, November 5, 1963.

- "The United States Print Media and its War on Psychedelic Research in the 1960s." Jessica M. Bracco, Buffalo State College, 2019.

- "Walter Pahnke, Ph.D. Thesis, Harvard Divinity School," 1963.

Locations

- Harvard Divinity School Library

- Harvard University Archives

- Herbert Vetter Papers, Harvard Divinity School Archives

- Julio Mario Santo Domingo Collection, Harvard Archives, Houghton Library

- Lamont Library, Harvard

- M.I.T. Department of Distinctive Collections – Aldous Huxley Lecture Series, "What a Piece of Work Is a Man"

- New York City Library, Archives

- Papers of Herb Kelman, David C. McClelland, Timothy Leary, Harvard Divinity School Archives

- Timothy Leary Papers

- Widener Library, Harvard

- Harvard Medical School Archives, Countway Library - Papers of Henry Beecher

Studies

- Concord Experiment
- Liddell, W., and H. Weil-Malherbe. "The Effects of Methedrine and Lysergic Acid Diethylamide on Mental Processes on the Blood Adrenaline Levels." Journal Neurological Psychiatry, 1953.
- Good Friday Experiment
- Harvard Psilocybin Project
- The Project of Psychedelic Law and Regulation (POPLAR) - Harvard Law School
- Harvard Law - Petrie-flom Center - Examine the Ethical, Legal, Social Implications of Psychedelic Research, Commerce, and Therapeutics
- "Timothy Leary and Associates, Papers," Harvard Archives #17168.

Additional References

- Alpert, Richard [Ram Dass]. Be Here Now. San Cristobal, NM: Lama Foundation, 1971.
- ———. Grist for the Mill. Santa Cruz, CA: Unity Press, 1977.
- ———. Journey of Awakening: A Meditator's Guidebook. Rev. ed. New York: Bantam, 1990. First published 1978.
- ———. "Letter to Nathan Pusey." Harvard Crimson, May 29, 1963.

- ———. The Only Dance There Is. Garden City, NY: Anchor, 1974. First published 1970.

- Chase, Alston. Harvard and the Unabomber: The Education of an American Terrorist. W. W. Norton & Company, 2003.

- Cheever, Susan. My Name Is Bill. Simon & Schuster, 2004.

- Clark, Walter Houston. Chemical Ecstasy: Psychedelic Drugs and Religion. Sheed and Ward, 1969.

- Cohen, Allen. The San Francisco Oracle—Facsimile Edition. Berkeley, CA: Regent Press, 1991.

- Cohen, Sidney. "Lysergic Acid Diethylamide: Side Effects and Complications." The Journal of Mental and Nervous Disease, vol. 130, no. 1 (1960): 30-40.

Video and Audio Appendix

Hyperlinks

Tim Ferriss Show

Tim Ferriss Show, December 29, 2022

https://tim.blog/2022/12/29/brian-c-muraresku-dr-mark-plotkin-transcript/

Wade Davis – Introduction to Project

Video link

https://youtu.be/ZGtdeTUJCzg

Into to Richard Alpert

Video link

https://youtu.be/lSexPKDST60

Being Ram Dass

Ram Dass

https://youtu.be/zRQmO1rBXJg

Reflections on the Zeitgeist of the Harvard Psilocybin Project

Gunther Weil

https://www.youtube.com/watch?v=Ef35IX5TGdk&t=1592s

Leary Barron and Tim Leary - 1959-1960

https://www.youtube.com/watch?v=e5av6wHug-0

The Harvard Psilocybin Project 1960-1963 - Fall 2023

https://www.youtube.com/watch?v=5wI4-Cqkvwg

Harvard in the Amazon - Mark Plotkin

https://www.youtube.com/watch?v=91X0UMLjn04

Return to Harvard – Frank Barron

Video link

https://youtu.be/0GK9VzhhWBc

Wade Davis on Richard Evans Schultes

https://www.youtube.com/watch?v=5wI4-Cqkvwg

Video by Mark Plokin on Richard Evans Schultes

https://www.youtube.com/watch?v=91X0UMLjn04

Rare Footage LSD Experiment – Dr. Sidney Cohen

https://youtu.be/glTB9vtNueQ

Good Friday Experiment – Susan Gervasi

https://www.youtube.com/watch?v=WEsWmpf6dgc

Audio portion of Timothy Leary Speaking at Harvard ReUnion

https://soundcloud.com/thebeezone/timothy-leary-and-ram-das-harvard-reunion-1983?si=35361e1d6d0a4737b419ebe7ee7879f3&utm_source=clipboard&utm_medium=text&utm_campaign=social_sharing

Ram Dass and Timothy Leary 'After Show'

https://youtu.be/eYs-qohH6O8?si=qHPCn6wxucxaqSPL

Jordan Peterson and Roland Griffiths

https://youtu.be/zlNti4uDMr0

Andrew Weil on the Harvard Psilocybin Project.

https://www.youtube.com/watch?v=BZyjIpQWJzo

Havard Quixotic Pursuit Social Relations Dep

https://youtu.be/w4IXnEpVpFY

Psychedelic Medicine: From Tradition to Science

https://www.youtube.com/watch?v=SwMHr43fTqE

www.ingramcontent.com/pod-product-compliance
Lightning Source LLC
Chambersburg PA
CBHW070556270326
41926CB00013B/2328